GW00337568

Fortress H:
The Early Years

Neil Haverson

Eastern Daily Press

From: Neil Haverson
Fortress H
Norfolk

To: The Publisher
Eastern Daily Press
Prospect House
Rouen Road
Norwich

August 28, 1997

Dear Sir,

   Re: Fortress H; The Early Years.

   Are you sure this is a good idea?

A collection of classics from Neil
Haverson's popular EDP column

Fortress H

Eastern Daily Press

From: Neil Haverson
Fortress H
Norfolk

To: The Publisher
Eastern Daily Press
Prospect House
Rouen Road
Norwich

August 25, 1997

Dear Sir,

Re: Fortress H; The Early Years.

You're **quite** sure?

Contents

Contents

From: Neil Haverson
Fortress H
Norfolk

To: The Publisher
Eastern Daily Press
Prospect House
Rouen Road
Norwich

August 25, 1997

Dear Sir,

Re: Fortress H; The Early Years.

Well if you **must**.

CHANGE IS AS GOOD AS A REST, THEY SAY

The trouble with small human alarm clocks is that you cannot set them to go off at what, to you, is a reasonable hour.

Add a bit of excitement to their metabolisms, throw in some eager anticipation and goodness knows at what time your day will dawn.

This particular Sunday it was 5.30 am, I leapt lethargically from my bed, blundered over a chair that we do not have, and crashed into a wall where there should have been a door. It was the first day of our holiday and I was attempting to perform a familiar task in unfamiliar surroundings. Such was the racket from the early risers that they did not hear my attempts in a semi-comatose state to extricate myself from the bedroom.

Finally, my eyelids agreed to part company enough to allow me to see and I burst into the Brats' room to shut them up. Unfortunately, the brain had not been notified that speech was required, so all that came out of my mouth was a sentence of slurred drivel.

"Shup! Juno whatimis?" Two pairs of round eyes stared at me in bewilderment. They hadn't come across this in the exploits of Billy Bluehat or Jennifer Yellowhat.

All responses from young persons in this situation commence the same way. "But daddy, we were only ...." a further word is then added according to the crime. Here is a selection: playing, painting, looking, stroking, strangling, delete as applicable.

We were at Hemsby, staying in one of the older-style bungalows, where Mrs H and I intended to re-create for our children the seaside holidays of our own childhood.

This was one chapter of the fairy tale that did not need re-telling. Something had to be done. Termination of the ice cream agreement was threatened, not to mention the withdrawal of the index-linked pocket money deal. This did have some effect and the pocket money remained intact, until we visited a toy shop in Yarmouth. Here, despite our best efforts to spend it on educational toys which would set them up for such things as a career in the City, it was squandered on a variety of seemingly useless bits of plastic. Not to mention a torch which later became the subject of a parental repossession order.

My sleep was disturbed by something else over which I had no control. At first light, every bird in the neighbourhood brought its head from under its wing and indulged in the feathered equivalent of jogging. This consisted of landing with a thump just above my head on the wooden roof, and scampering across it with a noise like a herd of stampeding buffalo. Unable to sleep, I lay there plotting ways to scupper their dawn landings. The best that I could come up with was to coat the roof with superglue.

I must admit that you do not seem to need so much sleep on holiday. The brain selects a lower gear so the human being is more easily refreshed. This is just as well because, at the other end of the day, things improved only because the birds were silent. Presumably they were in some avian infirmary having cartilage operations on their knees from all that heavy landing.

The Brats, on the other hand, dismissed sleep as a mere inconvenience in their quest for 24-hour fun. They pleaded fear of the dark in a strange room so, naively, we allowed them to take the torch to bed. When we investigated the soft glow under the sheets, we found an assortment of books, a football, a plastic sword and something sticky which looked as though it might once have been edible.

I suppose a change is as good as a rest, but it wasn't half nice to get back to work for a bit of peace and quiet.

WHO SAID CHEATS NEVER PROSPER?

All eyes are focused on Wembley today for the Cup Final. Few people realise that there is another footballing contest of equal intensity taking place. I am able to bring you details of the encounter, thanks only to an under-handed piece of cheque-book journalism.

The venue is not Wembley but the back garden of Fortress Haverson, and the game is a no-holds-barred struggle between me and Brat Minor, with the occasional intervention of Brat Major. Normal FA rules do not apply. For example, the match has gone on for several hours already, spanning a number of weekends. I am not altogether sure of the score at present, but goals scored have run into three figures apiece. Brat Minor has brought to the rules a flexibility not seen before in the game of football.

I thought there was a law which says that you must not handle the ball. Not according to the rule book of Brat Minor. If he falls over, he claims that it is fair play for him to hug the ball to his chest to stop me getting it. If, from my shot at goal, the ball goes in off the post, this constitutes a save by his goalkeeper. The same situation at the other end counts as a goal. The game may be stopped at any point where Brat Minor fancies a drink or if his fish fingers are ready. Play also tends to get suspended if I am threatening to score.

To date, all the many periods of the game have been played behind closed doors. This is to minimise crowd trouble. The situation is already tense with Brat Major persisting in invading the pitch on her bike. Already there have been a number of injuries, mostly to surrounding plants that seem intent on pushing through for a grandstand seat. Brat Minor usually gets injured when I am through his defence and confronted with an open goal. He goes down as if pole-axed. As I go to help him, he is up and away and I am another goal down.

At the end of the last session I lodged a formal complaint about the way he was, in my opinion, cheating. If the ball goes out behind the goal, he carries it back into play, drops it on the ground and wellies it into the goal. This is followed by a typical professional footballer's reaction to scoring. In order words, several noisy circuits of the garden, punching the air in triumph. He stops short of the hugging and kissing, probably because the only person on hand with whom to perform these acts is his sister.

All right, so my pride was injured just a bit. Upstaged by a six year old who undoubtedly goes into school on the Monday morning and provides an action replay of how he took his dad to the cleaners. With this in mind, and aware that I could still be shown a red card as I left the field, I accused the little hooligan of cheating. If he was going to tell all his mates at school how easily he defeated me then I would tell all my mates at work that he cheats.

This stopped him in his tracks. He turned to me wide-eyed and said "You're not going to put it in the paper are you?" I hadn't actually thought of that until he planted the idea in my mind. "You must not put it in the paper" he repeated emphatically. So here is the sleazy piece of cheque-book journalism.

I went for his weak spot. "I'll give you a Crunchie and a Milky Way if you'll let me write about it". He was wavering. I went in for the kill. "All right, I'll throw in some Rolos as well".

"Will I be able to eat them straight away? You won't put them in the cupboard and say they are for later like you usually do?" I agreed and we had a deal, and so I am able to bring you this exclusive.

Some time around ten o'clock tomorrow morning, after he has inserted a sufficient number of Weetabix in his stomach, play will resume. You will probably never know the result of the match. I cannot afford the chocolate bars to secure the rights.

HUSBANDS ARE THE FASHION VICTIMS

The journey of my toast from plate to eagerly awaiting mouth was halted by an excited yelp from Mrs H.

She was jabbing an agitated finger at the colour supplement that she was reading over Sunday breakfast. "Look, it's my coat," she exclaimed proudly. Pictured in the magazine was a group of ladies posing outside a stately home and indeed one of the set was wearing a coat identical to the one recently purchased by herself. Gosh, I thought, I'm married to a trend-setter. Stepping out in the fashions before they make the Sunday colour supplements. Then I realised that she had become silent and that the only thing breaking the peace was my crunching of the slice of toast liberally coated in marmalade.

I wasn't quite sure what to do next. I felt that some comment was expected so I fell back on one of the tried and tested responses. "Doesn't suit her as much as it suits you," I said smugly. To my amazement this did not produce the usual scoff of disbelief. It turned out that the article was one of those before and after pieces and the picture of the lady wearing Mrs H's coat was in the before shot. I should state with undue haste that that is no reflection on the pace with which Mrs H pursues fashion.

While fashions change, the level of the bank balance remains generally in decline and this dictates the time lag between the item being spotted on the catwalk, or more likely in the mail order catalogue, and its arrival in the Haverson wardrobe.

When it comes to clothes I have to admit that I am hopeless. I rely totally on Mrs H. I have gone solo in the past to buy things like shirts but my complete lack of any colour co-ordination has meant that the item has to be changed the following day for something more appropriate. This in turn has led to the withdrawal of any purchasing authority that I ever had as far as apparel is concerned and I just wear what turns up in the wardrobe. Even so, I have to report for daily inspection before leaving for work, in case I have dragged out that excessively wide, flowered tie of which I was so proud in the sixties.

Being void of fashion sense does have one major bonus. In general I am excused shopping for clothes with Mrs H. as my presence is of little value. My advice is nonetheless sought on the few occasions that I do accompany her on a sortie round the boutiques.

She will emerge from the fitting room wearing her chosen outfit. Firstly she will pose at all angles to seek confirmation from the mirror that the new dress disguises all those unwanted contours that even the most svelte females claim to have. Having completed this initial inspection, I am asked to participate in the ritual.

"Do you like it?"

"Yes, it's very nice."

"Do you really mean that? You'll say anything to get out of the shop. Does it really suit me?"

This can be a tricky one. If you are on some kind of suicide mission you could say; "Well it does make you look a bit big round the hips." You could be vague and say, "It suits your figure" but that is a dangerous one and could lead to further interrogation.

The situation doesn't end once the actual purchase has been made. Later that evening it's not unusual to find the prized garment neatly packed in its carrier bag. "It's no good," she'll say. "I m just not happy with it. It'll have to go back". Then comes the final payoff. "Here's the receipt. I wondered if you could just pop it back to the shop when you are in the city on Monday."

STRICKEN DOWN BY A VENGEFUL VIRUS

There is nothing like a good dose of flu to bring out the best in a chap in a crisis. Mrs H had just recovered from a particularly vengeful virus. It had all the constituents of a real belter of a bug. Shaking, sweating, headaches and the thing that always tells me that she is really ill, loss of appetite. If Mrs H ain't eating, she certainly ain't well.

Like a well-oiled machine I stepped in and took over the running of the domestic activities at Fortress Haverson. I will be the first to admit that things were not necessarily done in the conventional way. For example, why vacuum under the armchairs every time? Nobody spends any time there. And how many visitors arrive and make it a priority to check the tachometer on the Hoover? It's all down to time and motion. A little less motion will give you a bit more time.

I must confess that the trip to the supermarket was not as smooth as it might have been. I was given a list which should have made things easy but it wasn't as straightforward as that. What do you do if you are not sure if the packet you are clutching in your hand is the item marked on the list? Do you buy it and risk wasting money on something she never uses? Or do you err on the side of caution and not get it at all, at the risk of being told; "Well, that's that then. Even if I am better by the weekend I can't do Sunday dinner now."

Weights and measures are another weak point. How many slices of ham do you get for eight ounces? And the assistants will ask difficult questions when you ask for a pound of cheese. "It's a little bit over, sir. Is that all right?" It always seems to be a little bit over. Perhaps they are on an incentive bonus.

Generally things were going quite well until Brat Minor decided to test a chap's stamina and initiative. It was 4.15 in the morning when he decided to come out in sympathy with his mother and was promptly sick.

Semi-conscious, I staggered from bed and, even though I say it myself, proceeded to execute a slick operation of clearing up the mess and changing sheets and the little horror's pyjamas. Throughout this exercise Brat Minor jabbered away continuously giving me in graphic detail a blow by blow account of what he had just done.

As any parent knows, there is something in a child's metabolism which prevents them being sick just the once. They seem to save a bit for later. Having been caught like this before I applied forward planning to be one step ahead.

I placed in a strategic position by his bed a plastic bucket, giving him strict instructions to aim for it if he felt unwell again. Sure enough, just as I was tumbling into a great abyss of slumber, I became aware that I was being summoned urgently. About half an hour had elapsed and true to form he had done it again. I stared in disbelief. The only thing in close proximity to his bed that had entirely escaped the second instalment was the bucket.

After this I finally got to sleep. It seemed that I had been unconscious for a matter of minutes before the alarm was bleeping unsympathetically in my ear and I found myself downstairs preparing breakfast.

Catering was no problem. However, the items on the menu would not have stood up to close scrutiny, particularly if their nutritional value was to be examined. And I did overhear Brat Major confiding to her mother that "Mummy wouldn't let us have chocolate so close to dinner time."

When my temporary spell as foreman finished, I transferred back to labourer. But not for long. Soon it was my turn to take over the role of patient with the desperate cry of "Quick somebody, where's that bucket?"

BIRTH OF A
BAGGY JUMPER

It was an office that I do not usually have cause to enter in the course of my normal work so I was unfamiliar with the layout. I walked in somewhat hesitantly.

All was quiet with half a dozen people, heads down, hard at work. I spoke briefly to the person I had come to see and then, still slightly self-conscious, turned on my heel. I pulled open the door and swept out of the room. Straight into the darkness of a small cupboard.

I can assure you there is nothing you can say or do to minimise the embarrassment in such circumstances. I emerged from the gloom to be confronted by six quizzical faces. I babbled something about how on earth did they work in such heat, selected another door, checked carefully that it led to the outside world, and ran. I have not returned to that office since and keep my eyes dipped if I meet any of the incumbents in the corridor.

Nerves and stress make us do and say things that we would not normally contemplate. I remember when Brat Major was being born. I was there at the birth. Mrs H was lying on the bed with the action well under way when the sister suddenly said; "Now where's the foetal monitor?"

Inspired by nerves, I replied in a voice that had a hint of hysteria in it; "Please, Miss, can I be foetal monitor today?" The subsequent withering look was so powerful that it was almost enough to cancel the plans for the conception of Brat Minor.

Later during her labour, Mrs H unwittingly saved me from further embarrassment by preventing me making another stupid remark. Every time she had a painful contraction she had developed the habit of grabbing hold of my jumper and pulling hard. This caused me to assume suddenly a variety of ungainly positions.

Brat Major was showing a marked reluctance to join her anxious parents in the big world. So the mid-wife rolled up her sleeves to offer some encouragement. Like Nureyev lecturing a bunch of ballet students, she announced in haughty tones; "I am about to perform an episiotomy."

This begged a reply and in a split second several alternatives presented themselves in my brain for consideration. The thought of the sister springing athletically around the delivery room with an assortment of complicated movements was too much. Fortunately, nature intervened and I did not have time to put my foot in it.

As I engaged brain and opened my mouth, Mrs H had another contraction. She grabbed my jumper and yanked hard. I hurtled across the bed and landed on top of her like a wrestler going for a submission. My face ended up adjacent to the gas and air mask. Assisted by a couple of lungfuls of this I regained my equilibrium, by which time the sister was poised for action and my opportunity to be silly had passed.

Brat Major finally put in an appearance. While Mrs H was recovering, I was sent to the fathers' room. Already a grinning, self-satisfied new father was in there. Unlike me he was perfectly relaxed. He was using the telephone to inform his relatives of what, clearly to him, had been a single-handed triumph. "The cord was wrapped a couple of times round his neck. Soon sorted that out, though," he said, as if he had been on hand with his penknife to save the day.

Then in I walked. A sweating, harassed individual clothed in an extremely baggy jumper and looking as though I had just gone five rounds with Giant Haystacks.

FOR THE LOVE OF
A GOOD WOMAN

It seems widely accepted that children mature much earlier than they did years ago. When I was young the bow and arrow was used to emulate Robin Hood. It has been traded in by today's youngsters for the version that Cupid fires.

This was illustrated by Brat Minor the other day who, at the age of six, announced to the inmates of Fortress Haverson that he has no fewer than three girls in his class vying for his affections. Indeed, all three have expressed an intention to marry him. There is no need at this stage for a quiet parental word drawing his attention to the folly of getting mixed up with one woman, let alone three. He seems nonplussed by the whole situation.

He is, of course, quite right. When he reaches his teens, he may wish that he had retained his current preoccupation with Batman for a few years longer. Batman makes him feel as if he has power over everything in the universe. Let a woman in his life and our young caped crusader will find that there are things in life that just cannot be zapped.

He can put his Batman kit in the cupboard when he wants to do something else, but let him try telling his mates he can't play football with them because he is going for a walk in the park with a member of the opposite sex; or, worse still, being taken round the January sales. To date, Batman has played no part in persuading him to have a bath or submit willingly to having his hair washed. For strange things happen when a female begins to exert some influence.

In my younger days I shared a flat with three others. It was a typical male-dominated pad. We felt a good covering of dust added character to the place and the washing-up rota was, to say the least, flexible. A trip to the laundrette was on a par with a visit to the dentist. You didn't go until it really hurt.

Then we became aware that one of our number was disappearing after tea. We followed him one evening. His trail led us to a sporadically-used room in the flat, the bathroom. He was immersing himself in hot water every night and sneaking out with hair that had been brushed as if he was being exhibited at Crufts.

Yes, it was a female. A change came over him. On such occasions when he could find time to join his flatmates at the pub, he downgraded his drinking from pints to halves. The musty smell of the flat, a mixture of questionable cooking and a lack of opening of the windows, was tempered with a new aroma. Aftershave had found its way into our pit.

Things went downhill for him from then on. Under her influence he began to eat properly and his complexion cleared up. He discovered that steak and kidney pie does not come exclusively out of a Fray Bentos tin. The spin-off effect on us was that the odd home-made cake used to find its way into our larder, an added bonus to our staple diet of an infinite number of pieces of toast.

Of course, this started the rot. Before we knew it, another of the fold began showing the tell-tale signs of excessive cleanliness and was actually caught pressing his trousers. The next thing we knew, his fashion sense had been plucked from the previous decade and he looked like a walking advert for a mail order catalogue.

When the time comes, these tales must be told to Brat Minor to prepare him for what is ahead. I bet Batman drinks pints.

TIME IS ALL TAKEN
UP IN MY BOOK

I attended a time management course the other day. All good stuff: how to get your in-tray empty and your out-tray full. Rather knocks on the head my general criteria for life which is never do today what you can put off until tomorrow.

One suggestion from the course tutor was that we should keep a notebook beside our bed for a "to do" list. If I did this, I rather fancy that most of the entries would be in Mrs H's handwriting. At Fortress Haverson my time is well managed for me by both Mrs H and the Brats.

So aware is Mrs H of my downtime that she can see round corners. In fact, not only round corners but from the bedroom, down the stairs along the hall and into the lounge. The moment I am about to hit the armchair her voice drifts into my life with "could you just do ..."

Mrs H is a master of the could-you-just-do job. The "could you just" part is to minimise the enormity of the actual task. It lulls you into a false sense of security, making you think that she is only going to ask you to turn on the light. In fact it's more like: "Before you go to hockey, could you just re-lay the patio?"

It never ceases to amaze me how, if I do make a determined effort to do some jobs at home, I can select the wrong task. She will go out shopping while I attack the garden. I will dig the whole lot, mow the lawn, sow vegetables, plant flowers, prune roses and creosote the fence.

There I am exhausted, battle scarred with soil stains from a bit of good honest toil and what are her first words when she gets home? "On a nice day like this I really thought that you would have taken the opportunity to paint the door. It's supposed to rain tomorrow, now you won't be able to do it until next weekend."

Unable to persuade the vocal chords to jangle, I become like a bewildered goldfish. With jaws opening and closing silently, I wave a tired arm in the general direction of a garden that has just been transformed.

This does not have the desired effect. Spotting the freshly dug soil there is a swift inspection. "What happened to that fuchsia my mother planted in the corner? You've dug it up haven't you? You thought it was a weed didn't you? She's coming up on Sunday. You'd better get another one and plant it quickly."

I know that she is not undermining my efforts on the garden; she is just applying that thing known as female logic. I would explain it to you - but I don't understand it.

My performance with fork and shears takes a further step into the background. She discovers that Brats have been amalgamating water and soil and have achieved notable success in producing mud. The fruits of their labours can be found in most places where it is necessary to walk. At some stage during the morning, one or both Brats have found the need to go indoors to take on board refreshment. This is evident from the trail of footprints leading to and from the fridge.

This, of course, is also my fault. I try to point out that the eye in the back of my head, sadly was not functioning. It is not easy to maintain supervision of that devious pair when you are halfway up an apple tree clinging on for dear life while trying to saw off a branch the size of a telegraph pole.

"Where on earth do you think I am going to find the time to clear up this mess?" she exclaims.

Perhaps I could make a suggestion here, dear. Have you ever thought about doing a course in time management?

FACING UP TO
TIME'S PASSING

The carrot of not having to shave each day is almost enough to give me the courage to defy Mrs H's veto on me growing a beard.

I hate shaving. I have one of those beards that puts up quite a fight. I have tried all the blades on the market. The double-edged, super flexible, move with the lumps and bumps on the terrain of your face razors all leave me with a scattering of tiny dots of blood. I look like an Ordnance Survey map in draft form.

When I present myself for daily inspection before leaving for work, Mrs H has to check that there is no trickle of blood running down my shirt collar. People might think that we had had a fight, or that I had been a victim of the deadly aim of Brat Minor with his Ghostbusters' popper gun.

This daily confrontation with the mirror does mean that the memory gets updated each day with the latest view of the facial features. This, in turn, means that any gradual changes such as the ageing process pass almost unnoticed. One can get used to the idea that there has been no perceptible change since one was nineteen.

Fortunately, or otherwise, something will usually pop up to remind you that such things as passing years, not to mention a couple of taxing Brats, manifest themselves in the form of the odd wrinkle and a belt with more than one used notch.

The other day, Mrs H and I watched a short cine film taken at our wedding. It had lain, untouched, in a cupboard for many years - not because we did not want to be reminded of the event, but because we don't have a projector to show it. We have had it transferred to a video and the other day we sat in stunned silence watching, among other things, friends and relatives who are now attending that great ceremony in the sky.

A couple of heckling Brats did not help soften the blow. Who, they asked, is that slim chap with the rather long hair wearing the flared suit? That, I croaked in reply, is your father. After this frightening fact had sunk in, I got the impression that, had they been older, they would have demanded sight of their birth certificates to substantiate this. Clearly this was a stigma that, until now, they had been unaware would be attached to them for the rest of their lives.

It was my turn to smile when a lady in white who, to be honest, could have done with shedding a pound or two at the time, emerged from a large car, to be identified as the future Mrs H. The film was shot entirely outside the church. The service itself remains to me a blur, with the exception of one incident that I

At the rehearsal, the vicar impressed one point on Mrs H, or Miss H as she was then. "When, during the marriage ceremony, I extend my right hand, I want your right hand. If you offer me your left hand I shall ignore it. We shall stand there until you give me your right hand." This became ingrained on Mrs H's brain. When we finished signing the first hymn, the vicar extended his right hand. Instantly, Mrs H shot out her right in response and grabbed the vicar's hand in a vice-like grip.

There followed a pause which seemed to last an age as the reverend gentleman and Mrs H defiantly held each other's eye. The tension was unbearable. I could hear a puzzled congregation shuffling nervously. Just as I was beginning to think that she was showing preference to marry the vicar rather than me, the bemused parson hissed at her through clenched teeth; "I only want your hymn sheet!"

MEAN TIME CAUGHT
US OUT AGAIN

As we left for Sunday lunch at the in-laws last weekend, I glanced at the clock. As expected, we were precisely one hour later in leaving than we had intended to be.

I know what you're thinking; it was the weekend when the clocks went forward and we had not allowed for the lost hour. Not so. The previous evening I had dutifully done the rounds of the clocks, including the one on the cooker. This particular timepiece is done with great care ever since, in the process of one equinox adjustment, I unwittingly activated the automatic timer. We wondered why the oven wouldn't work. Then we woke up to a warm kitchen and discovered that the cooker had come to life in the early hours.

So, why were we an hour late last Sunday? Well, to us, Greenwich Mean Time and British Summer Time serve only as a starting point. At Fortress Haverson the sun rises and sets according to time set by Mrs H. Last Sunday we were, as usual, in our own little time warp.

For some reason, as we bustle around, I always become convinced that we are running on schedule. The Brats had been persuaded that they could not take with them every toy that they possess. They had been prised out of red wellies and Batman tee-shirts and forced into something a bit more suitable for Sunday lunch.

I had been told that the chosen shirt looked awful with the chosen trousers. I changed the trousers only to be told that I should have changed the shirt. I then changed the trousers and the shirt. At the re-inspection I was dismissed with the "Oh it's not ideal but you'll have to do" comment.

I loaded the car, read the paper and, in case there was time to cut the hedge, checked on the progress of Mrs H. She seemed to be no further ahead than when I had last seen her at least half an hour before. "Shall I wear the blouse and skirt or that dress?" She asked as if time was actually standing still.

"Wear that blouse and skirt," I replied instantly, hoping that my prompt decision would inspire equally prompt action. As I suspected, my advice had been sought only to confirm what she had already decided. "I think I'll wear the dress", she declared. "Now go away and let me get on. I've only got to change and do my hair and I'm ready." I knew what "only got to do" meant so I vanished for a further 20 minutes.

After this time, I could contain myself no longer so I paid another visit to see just what she was doing. There she was wearing, guess what, the blouse and skirt. "I tried the dress but it makes me look fat." Fancy blaming the poor old dress for that.

I was at last given leave to round up the Brats and board the car as she would be "just a minute". We were strapped in awaiting clearance for take-off. After a few further minutes my dear co-pilot strode across the tarmac. Yes, you've guessed it, she was back in the dress now. A button had been discovered missing from a vital part of the blouse "so I'll just have to look fat". Brat Major opened her mouth but a piercing look from me nipped in the bud her assessment of her mother's figure.

We were 55 minutes late as we sped off up the road. At this point any of our neighbours can tell you what happened next as it seems to happen every time there is a mass exodus from Fortress Haverson. Within 30 seconds we re-appeared round the corner and screamed to a halt in the drive. Yours truly leaped out, rushed into the house and returned clutching Brat Minor's plastic sword. For him, to be exposed without his sword is like arriving at the check-out without your wallet.

Off we go again, up the road, round the corner, then it's, "You did lock the back door didn't you?"

Aaaaghhh!

A WIFE ALOOF
FROM WASHING

Mrs H's lower jaw dropped - and stayed there. This jaw, one of a matching pair, usually operates with consummate ease. Its rapid movements freely dispense advice to me and the Brats on how we may strive for perfection. Before becoming stationary, the jaw had contributed towards her making the staggered utterance; "Have you really finished? Does it work?"

The car door handle had broken. Not only had I, who am to DIY what the M25 is to carefree motoring, visited the garage and purchased the correct part at the first attempt, but I had removed the old one and fitted the new one with no more than a small scratch on the paint work and minor lacerations to the index finger. What's more, this half-hour job had taken me little over two hours to complete. For me, this is on a par with breaking the four-minute mile barrier.

Past experience of my self-confessed ineptitude meant that Mrs H would only be convinced of my achievement once she had seen my efforts with her own eyes. As she peered incredulously at the completed job, I could not resist my usual sarcastic comment that I invariably make when she is anywhere near the car.

"Have you noticed that the fairies have paid another visit and cleaned the car?" I inquired. This was greeted with the usual reply of who was going to do the washing and cook the dinner while she was out here cleaning the car?

As she also drives the thing I have issued an open invitation to her to take part in some of the routine maintenance tasks. She is cordially invited to attend such ceremonies as the checking of the oil and the topping up of the radiator. Not to mention the checking of the tyre pressures followed by the twenty-minute search in the gravel to find the valve dust cap when you have finished.

Last weekend I made great play of getting out the car cleaning equipment; excessive rattling of the bucket; much grunting and heaving over connecting the hose. I was about to admit defeat and turn on the hose when the Brats suddenly appeared, kitted out in wellies and ready for action. "Mummy says that she will give us extra pocket money if we clean the car". It transpired that they had negotiated better terms than I enjoy. Not only was there payment, but built into the agreement was a chocolate incentive bonus.

Brat Major set about her task with vigour as if further enhancements were on offer if she finished the job the same day. Brat Minor, on the other hand, provided confirmation that no way is he ever going to suffer from ulcers. Adopting the economic approach to expending effort, he selected a piece of car, made himself comfortable and spent several minutes gently polishing it. When I suggested that he might vary the bit of metal that was his focus of attention, he immediately asked if acceptance of such a suggestion would result in an upward revision of the payment conditions.

When the answer was no, he decided to turn his attention to doing a bit of hosing. His efforts put me in mind of those frantic days of trying to toilet-train him. No matter where I stood I received a liberal spraying. Accusations that he was doing it on purpose almost brought about a total withdrawal of labour by both Brats. They only resumed work when I agreed to top up their already lucrative deal.

When we had finished, Mrs H appeared on the scene. She walked up to the shining vehicle and examined one of the doors. She looked up and our eyes met. For the first time since I can't remember when, I do believe the look on my face actually silenced her. Perhaps I do her a dis-service. Perhaps she wasn't going to say; "Oh look. You've missed a bit."

SO THIS IS WHAT THEY CALL THE OFF-SEASON

I have just completed a hockey season unique in my playing career. We have staggered on to the field almost every Saturday since last September, finishing up at the end of April with a 100 per cent record: we didn't win a game.

The club is called Carrow. We were on the verge of changing the name to Carrow Nil as this was what appeared in the results column of the EDP each Tuesday. However, in an unguarded moment, an over-generous opposition defence allowed us to score. Indeed there were even occasions when we looked as though we might win but, inevitably, in the last few minutes, we managed to snatch defeat from the jaws of victory.

I cannot say that there was too much sympathy coming from the inmates of Fortress Haverson. In the early part of the season the Brats would greet my arrival home with, "How did you get on today, Dad?" As time wore on this was moderated to "How many did you lose by today, Dad?" Eventually no inquiry at all was forthcoming. My efforts to generate some interest in the latest defeat were met with, "Be quiet Dad. We're watching Jim'll Fix It."

The end of the season is an emotional time. Mrs H weeps with joy at the prospect of no more muddy kit to wash. She is always happy to wash my gear but has one golden rule; she considers that I am a big boy now and should be able to remember to put it in the laundry basket. Unfortunately for my team mates who have to change with me this is not always the case.

The end of the season means no more banter with the lads, no more post-match pint but, worst of all, it means that I am on hand at Fortress Haverson for a few extra hours each week. Mrs H and I view the same situation from two entirely different perspectives. I maintain that Saturday afternoons are for hockey but that, in the close season I may, just may, be available for other duties. Mrs H considers that Saturday afternoons are for the "could you just do" jobs and that it is only by generous consent that I am let out to play during the winter months.

Last Saturday was the first fixture-less weekend. I strolled down for a leisurely breakfast and found in the kitchen an aide memoir in the handwriting of Mrs H. It was placed in such a way that I couldn't miss it. And it was headed "Neil". Now, this is rather like walking into your boss's office when he isn't there and finding your personal file on his desk. You're dying to know what's in it but on the other hand you may read something that it's better that you don't know. Such as the fact that you are about to become a former employee.

Curiosity got the better of me and I read on. It was indeed a "could you just do" list and was written in Mrs H's own version of shorthand. "Do vac" was Top of the list. The full version of this is; test vacuum cleaner, diagnose fault, effect repair, re-test machine. There is, however, a twist in the last bit. Re-test machine in fact means, "since you have it plugged in and running, Hoover the lounge and bedrooms while you're at it."

"Stick Brat Minor's sword" was next. This is a job that I have been meaning to do for months - stick it in the bin. With this weapon, the would-be knight has inflicted a number of wounds on his sister, reduced the cat to a nervous wreck and damaged any object that happened to get in the way of his swashbuckling.

The word "mend" appeared on the list a number of times. This word is a simple prefix to a monumental task. It's rather like the chief engineer arriving at Heathrow Airport on a Monday morning to find a note which says "mend Concorde".

Oh, roll on September.

PEDAL POWER OVER GRAVITY

It's not unusual to sustain a grazed shin from stumbling over an abandoned Brat-sized bicycle when wandering around the back garden of Fortress Haverson.

In spite of my constant nagging neither Brat seems capable of standing up his or her bicycle. Instead, when something more attractive comes along which supersedes the desire to ride a bicycle, the unfortunate machines are just dumped.

The other weekend, as I came round the corner of the house, I was confronted by Brat Major pedalling furiously on a course that was going to result in damage to one or both of us. As I emerged from the shrubbery, she complained that the confines of the garden were not sufficient to exploit the full potential of her bike. And how about a bike ride? In fact, with a number of challenging "could you just do" jobs approaching through the back door in the form of Mrs H, it seemed by far the lesser of two evils.

Things took a turn for the worse when Brat Minor overheard and demanded a bike ride, too. He had not, until then, inflicted himself on an unsuspecting highway, so this meant that I had to go twice as there was no way that I would be able to control both of them at once.

What a sight it was, me on my ancient bike. The sort you see in period drama such as Miss Marple. Only the wheels point in the direction in which you are going. The saddle is angled to the left and the handlebars to the right.

Brat Major was first. She is quite accomplished on her bike and was little trouble apart from the lapses in concentration when she spotted an acquaintance and could not control the need to issue a vociferous, arm-waving greeting.

Brat Minor on his tiny bike took several revolutions of the pedals to propel himself forward any distance at all. His little legs pumped away like fury in an effort to keep up with me. Add to this a rattling mudguard and a little boy who used every available spare breath to provide a running commentary, and you can begin to appreciate some of the atmosphere of this strange outing.

I, on the other hand, was pedalling so slowly, to give him a chance, that the peculiar assembly of my machine was exaggerated and it looked as if I was desperately fighting a losing battle to turn left all the time.

Brat Minor had to pedal with such intensity that he negotiated the entire journey while performing a permanent speed wobble. In spite of this, he maintained a reasonably straight line. Until, that is, he came across an obstruction such as a parked car.

"Pull out to avoid the car," I said gently so as not to worry him. "Move over to miss that car," I repeated with a degree of urgency creeping into my voice. "Pull out!" I screamed as he wobbled erratically within inches of a shining BMW. Simultaneously, half a dozen heads popped up over garden fences, all distracted from horticultural labours by the commotion in an otherwise peaceful road. Fortunately, none of these heads belonged to the owner of the BMW.

After they had drunk in this vista of an hysterical father on a bike which had clearly been assembled to emulate the movements of a lame crab, and a small boy who seemed to be under the delusion that he was performing in the Tour de France, they decided it was better not to look.

Quantity rather than quality is important to children, so Brat Minor had to be taken exactly the same distance as Brat Major. Therefore, for around a mile and a half, he was locked in a desperate battle with gravity.

Finally, on return to Fortress Haverson, both Brat and bike were grounded, the former looking the worse for wear. Actually, as Mrs H was not backward in coming forward to point out, his father was not in good shape either.

FRANKLY DEAR, I DON'T GIVE A DAMN

I really must be brave, grasp the nettle as they say, and introduce some new time-keeping rules at Fortress Haverson.

The problem is that I am one of those people who, if they say that they will be there at 8 o'clock then they are there at 8 o'clock. If I'm not, then there is a good reason why not. The rest of the inmates, as I have mentioned before, do not regulate their activities to the passage of time.

The Brats will respond only if there is a pecuniary advantage or if something sweet and sickly is on offer should they be able to make themselves available at the appointed hour. With Mrs H it is even worse: I cannot afford to pay her to be ready on time. Plying her with goodies only arouses unnecessary suspicion, followed by intense questioning should I hint at the need for a late pass for the weekend.

I have tried lying about the time we are supposed to be at a function. For example, if we are due to be there at 8 o'clock, I tell her that it is imperative that we are there at 7.30. This does not mean that we will be there by 7.30 but it does mean that we are in with a fighting chance of arriving by 8.15. This minor deception did have some effect, until she twigged what was going on. I think what gave it away was that everybody is used to the Haversons arriving late, so when we did arrive at 8.15, only a quarter of an hour late, everybody said in surprise, "Oh, you're early", so my scam was exposed.

The first new rule that I will introduce will be concerning the start of a television programme. All those wishing to view must be there at the start. If they are not then I will not undertake to bring them up to date with the plot. I will continue to give the five minute warning that the previous programme is finishing and that all those interested should take their seats. The times I have told Mrs H that something is about to get underway and I get the "I am now coming" call from the kitchen. By the time she arrives characters have been introduced and the plot has unfolded.

The annoying thing is that she breezes in while I am trying to concentrate and launches into a speech about something or other. "Do you know, I just had to stop the washing machine. The blue in the new blouse was running. It says it's machine washable ..."

"Are we going to watch this or what?" If I don't stop her, there will be another murder committed in the play and we shall never catch up. I then launch into my précis of the story so far:

"The man with the moustache is married to the blonde-haired girl who looks like the one that works on the bacon counter at the supermarket. She is having an affair with the gardener. The next door neighbour, who breeds snakes, has found out about it and told the vicar. The man with the moustache discovered that the vicar knows and has shot him." Everything is then repeated; "Ah, so the man with the moustache is having an affair with the vicar who looks like a piece of bacon. The blond gardener found a snake which he gave to the next door neighbour who shot it." I then spend the next few minutes correcting all this by which time the plot has considerably advanced and we give up and watch a video.

The situation is even worse if I am not at home and Mrs H decides to watch something. She so rarely sees the first ten minutes of anything that, if we do start to watch something together, she will suddenly say, just as I am getting interested, "Oh I have seen this. It's the one where the wife pushes her husband off the cliff." Fine, so there is no point in me watching it either now.

Watching a video is even worse. At least with a programme on television she has to be there at some stage or she will miss the lot. With a video it doesn't have to start until she gets there. And it has got a pause button for short interludes while she suddenly vanishes to do such things as "quickly wash my hair". Goodness knows how long it would take us to watch Gone with the Wind.

MAKING THE WRONG RESPONSE

Of all the things that I have written about her in this column, I suppose there could, just could, be the odd point with which Mrs H may wish to take issue. There is one small item that I can mention where I have every confidence that I will go unchallenged. In fact it applies to most women but Mrs H is among the leaders of the pack.

When it comes to talking there are few who can out-gun Mrs H. I realise that this public revelation may finally condemn me to life in the garage but she may well shrug it off with a wry smile if for no other reason than she knows the number of witnesses that could be called for the prosecution. I am prompted to mention it at this time because last week I met only the third living person with whom even Mrs H would have to book a talk slot.

Over the years I have gained quite a skill at appearing to listen while in fact concentrating on something else, such as a football match on the television. I have developed an uncanny instinct of knowing when even she may need to pause to take on board further oxygen. At these pit-stops I slip in one of a number of tried and tested phrases to give credence to the belief that I m riveted. "Really dear? ... did you dear? ... I really would write and complain ...".

I have been caught out when she has popped in a question. The set response of "that's awful dear" falls well short when the question was; "Do you like that new dress I bought on Saturday?" This prompts the words that most men hear at least once a week. "You haven't heard a word I've said. You're not listening."

"I am. I thought I heard one of the children calling and that distracted me." If in doubt, blame a Brat.

When I say that women talk more than men I don't think they cover any more topics than men. It's that they surround the subject with superfluous information and deviate from the point. For example a simple question like; "How old is Fred?" could bring a response like this.

"It's funny you should mention that. We were at a party he was at. He was with his first wife. She was a redhead. Had lovely earrings. I've seen them in the shops. Of course I can't wear that style not with my hair this short. Do you know, when I last had it cut, I said to the hairdresser ...." The original question has long since been buried in something more juicy.

I was relieved the other day to hear someone describing on the radio a situation that I had thought was peculiar to Fortress Haverson. It's that time of day when not only do I have the opportunity to talk but I am actually requested to do so. It is usually around 11 o'clock at night. Having got ready for bed in the shortest time possible, I am between the sheets, ensconced in a book. Mrs H, meanwhile, is performing all those exclusively feminine, time - consuming activities without which sleep cannot even be contemplated.

In the midst of slapping some cream or other on to a particular part of the body, she will utter the dreaded words; "Talk to me". There is nothing more guaranteed to erase from my brain any topic of conversation. I dry up. Having desperately read a few more paragraphs of my book, the best that I can do is; "What about?" This always causes annoyance and brings the reply; "Anything; just talk to me."

As she produces another tube of preservatives, I will dredge something from the depths of my mind. "I forgot to cancel the milk this morning." That does it. "Can't you find something romantic to say to your own wife?"?

You didn't mind me telling the nice readers this did you dear? Dear? Talk to me.

VET FIXED THE CAT AND MY WIFE'S CAR

My knowledge of the workings of the motor car are scant. However, if my move to the garage comes off, I shall have ample opportunity to become more familiar with the mysteries of the internal combustion engine. I do claim to have slightly more knowledge than a former colleague who thought that there was no need to top up the oil until that helpful light on the dashboard glowed.

All drivers at some time or other have been let down by their chariots. Usually this happens in one of two places, which are at opposite ends of the motoring spectrum. Either it is at a busy roundabout, causing absolute chaos, or on a remote country lane miles from the nearest telephone.

There is only one person I know who has a knack of breaking down and ends up with a posse of mechanics who happen to be nearby waiting for such an event. That is, of course, Mrs H.

Look at her track record. The engine wouldn't start in the supermarket car park. The lad collecting the trolleys came wandering by and just happened to know about cars, diagnosed the fault and put it right. The same thing happened in the middle of the village. From a nearby shop, no fewer than three people appeared and got it on the road again.

What happened a couple of weeks ago makes me think that this is no fluke; that this is some kind of skill that she has developed. While she was retrieving through the passenger door that Pandora's box known as a handbag, the door shut before she could grab the keys off the seat. It's an awful feeling when you do this. I know, I've done it. Not locked my handbag in the car, that is, just my keys.

Help was on hand for the ill-fated Mrs H. Just yards from where she was stranded there had been a small fire. Not only was there a fire engine there with its crew, but the police were in attendance too. Even then she almost blew it my saying "Excuse me constable" to a fireman.

The owner of the local greengrocers appeared from nowhere

with a suitable piece of wire and in no time Mrs H was on her way. Is she content with this? Indeed not. The very next day tested her skill again. This time she was taking the cat to the vet's when she had a flat tyre. Does she get stuck in the middle of nowhere like you and me? Of course not. The tyre showed the utmost consideration by waiting until she had parked at the vet's then announced its deflation by gently hissing. It was at this point that Mrs H turned the skill into an art.

"When you've looked at the cat," she said to the vet, "would you mind just having a look at my tyre and telling me whether I have got a puncture?" The vet accompanied Mrs H to the car park and was astute enough to spot that the tyre was flat and confirmed that there was every possibility that she has got a puncture.

Now I ask you, what could the poor chap do now that he had been lured into the car park? He could hardly do a James Herriot and bury his arm in the nearest cow and claim he couldn't lend a hand. His was trapped into changing the wheel. At least he was on the spot.

What I fear most is the phone call at work. A pathetic voice says "The car won't start". There invariably follows a tense exchange while I run through the procedures for starting a car. Each point is greeted with "Of course. I've done that. Do you think I'm stupid?"

Next she will try and describe the sound it makes when she attempts to start it. As she is making a noise down the phone like an overloaded washing machine, I know it is time to give in and go to the rescue. And guess what? Every time it has happened, the wretched thing has started at the first turn of the key when I arrive on the scene.

Perhaps it's time I got something more reliable. Car, that is, not wife.

AN OFFER MRS H HAD
TO REFUSE

Now look. Let me correct any wrong impressions that you may have of what I think of Mrs H. She is a real brick. She toils away at Fortress Haverson marshalling the Brats and looking after our well being. So much so that she makes me feel quite guilty. Take the other Saturday, for instance.

"Would you like a cup of coffee?" I enquired of her as I heaped the freeze-dried granules into my mug. As soon as I had uttered the words I regretted it. A total lapse in concentration, not to mention the spontaneous gesture of offering to make my good lady a beverage, had left the way open for the old guilt complex.

"No thanks," she replied, "I am too busy". I knew what was coming next. I had got the point but as usual the message had to be reinforced with the swift run down of all the jobs she had to do. "I'd love one but I just haven't got the time to stop."

By now I was heading towards the table with the newspaper under my arm and steaming mug in hand. As I sat down so the list of tasks was revealed. "I've got to put a load of washing in the machine, do the bedrooms, clean the bathroom, if I don't do some cooking today I shan't be able to do any till next weekend and you'll be the first to complain if there is nothing for tea tomorrow night. If you make me a cup of coffee, it will only stand there and get cold."

Having delivered this statement, Mrs H then went up a gear. She hurtled around the room at a tremendous pace to add credence to her argument that there really ought to be more than 24 hours in a housewife's day. And you can bet your life that whatever she is doing involves some form of frenzied activity in the vicinity of where I am imbibing.

"You'll have to just move a minute so I can get to the window. I must open it, it's so hot working in here".

I was not in the best of humour. I had just come in from the garden having cut the lawn with an obstinate mower that seems to suffer from hay fever. Awaiting me, following my sustenance, are a number of truculent weeds that will resolutely defend their right to remain in some of the heaviest soil ever to be threatened with a fork.

But it was too late. My guilty conscience was exposed. The situation in the kitchen was deteriorating fast. "Look," I said in a voice that I have to admit did lack a certain amount of conviction, "let me help you with some of this."

"No, you've got your own things to do," replied Mrs H, adding "just get on and drink your coffee." That did it. Ev en though I've made the same mistake before I always fall into the trap. I leapt up saying something like, "It's all right, it doesn't matter. I can do the garden anytime." With that, in a dramatic fashion, I flung the entire contents of my mug down the sink and with a look of defiance pledged myself to pull toward the common good of Fortress Haverson for the rest of the daylight hours. And beyond if necessary.

There was a glint of "you men are so predictable" in Mrs H's eyes as I rose to the bait and gobbled it down in its entirety. "Why did you do that?" she enquired calmly, knowing that victory was complete. "What a waste of coffee."

At this point relations degenerate somewhat. One of these days I will keep a cool head and gently sip my coffee as she rattles off the list of jobs she has to do. I will make sympathetic noises as she reveals the true horror of her lot. "Really dear? Have you got all that to do before bedtime? Is there anything I or our sweet children can do to lighten your load? It will be the talk of the village if it gets out that you have not Hoovered the bedrooms this weekend."

Assuming that she does not detect any hint of sarcasm in this response, there is just one danger with this approach. I may well suddenly find myself clutching a pack of Flash and a J-Cloth.

RANKING BENEATH
THIRSTY TOMATOES

As the mouth-watering smell of the burgers wafted from the barbecue, Mrs H was basking in the waves of sympathy from some of the other partygoers at what a long-suffering person she is, putting up with life at Fortress Haverson and that awful husband of hers.

For once, support was at hand. Just two days previously the hostess of the aforementioned barbecue had been within the portals of Fortress Haverson and seen at first hand where that "awful husband" comes in the pecking order. I asked for her verdict as to where she thought I fell in order of priority. "Neil," she said, "you certainly are last. Even I come before you." I set before you the facts as witnessed by our friend Sally. You may judge for yourself.

I arrived home from a hard day's slog with a stomach that was audibly making known its desire for food. As Sally arrived, I was asking for an estimated time of arrival of tea. My query was met with an instant response. "Could you just water the tomatoes? They'll die if you don't." That was not the answer I was looking for, and anyway would they die if only I did not water them? What would happen if she did not water them? Would the tomatoes understand the incredible pressure she was under managing the affairs of Fortress Haverson and cling to life until yours truly arrived with the watering can?

Like a lamb, I departed with a full watering can and returned, having dispensed the contents over the tomatoes which showed not a modicum of gratitude. "Anything I can do to help with tea?" I piped up bravely. "Could you just come with us to feed next door's rabbit?" The neighbours were on holiday and we were in charge of their menagerie. One of these rabbits can be an ugly brute and is known to bite the hand that feeds. It has to be held at bay by one person while the other hastily inserts the bowl of food into the run.

Back home and I opened my mouth to mention food, but Mrs H was too quick for me this time. "Could you just get the children to hurry up and get ready for bed."

"But, like me, they haven't had their tea yet." I pointed out. Not a hint of sarcasm in my voice.

"Oh, so they haven't. I cooked for them at lunch-time so could you just get them a sandwich? Sally, would you like a cup of coffee?" That'll set my meal back once those two get gassing over a cup of coffee. I attended to the Brats' every need and, with Herculean efforts, I, single-handed, got them to bed.

So, let's pause fo r a minute and see where I fall in the pecking order so far. The tomatoes have received life-saving nourishment, the rabbits are replete and the Brats are fed and watered. Even Sally has been granted a cup of coffee. But me? The stomach rumbles on.

A stroke of luck. Both the females paused for breath at the same time so I managed, with a pathetic voice now weak from hunger, to get in a desperate request for grub. "As it's so late now, we'll have some of that fish you bake in the oven. I've put the oven on, could you just put the fish in when it's up to temperature while I finish sorting this out with Sally?" This is a thinly-disguised way of saying if we are going to eat before bedtime you'll have to do it.

By the time we sat down to eat, even the sun had given up hope of seeing a meal on the table at Fortress Haverson and retired over the horizon. A smirking Sally bid us bon appetit and left while I gobbled down my food.

"Oh you've finished," observed Mrs H who was only halfway through her plateful. "You must have been hungry." To have finished so quickly was my final mistake of the evening. "Could you just do the washing up?"

FAIRIES OF TEETH,
ALE AND WALLETS

Brat Minor has begun dispensing his first set of teeth with monotonous regularity. I think his sister may be assisting with the removal of his molars in an effort to cash in on the tooth fairy.

From the tales he brings back from school, it appears that said fairy is well and truly index-linked. Not only have his chums received much more than the traditional sixpence, but also a variety of edible goodies guaranteed to drive a few more teeth to extraction.

Another fairy operates within the walls of Fortress Haverson. This is the wallet fairy. The wallet fairy differs from the tooth fairy in that she takes money rather than leaves it. She also makes lightning raids without informing the wallet-owner. There you are lads, that's why I never have any money when you catch me at the bar. The particular wallet fairy in question had a birthday recently. I shall not tell you how old she is, but let's just say that she got rather a lot of sympathetic cards drawing her attention to the advancing years.

With a distinct lack of forethought, I offered, as the big day fell on a Sunday, to take over the entire domestic running of Fortress Haverson, on the understanding that there should be no recrimination because the lawn wasn't cut. As I slaved away, assisted by two remarkably co-operative Brats, I wondered what all the fuss was about. Running the kitchen was a piece of cake. In fact we made one, cake that is, to celebrate the passing of another year in the life of Mrs H. I still won't tell you how old she is, but let's just say that we all perspired freely in the intense heat generated by the candles on the cake.

It stood me in good stead because, as I write, I am in an otherwise deserted Fortress Haverson. Just a few days ago, Mrs H packed her bags and left. The Brats have gone with her. I know what you are thinking. Sensible woman, should have done it years ago. At last she has left the blighter. Here's the twist. She's coming back soon. She has gone to stay with her father for a few days.

I am in charge. Daily orders have been put on hold and general Fortress policy waived. I can go to bed when I like, eat the last chocolate biscuit without feeling guilty and leave the washing-up to the next morning. I can spread myself about the bed, no elbow in the back to get me to move over, and no semi-conscious struggle to hang on to my share of the bed-clothes. I arrive home from work and no-one drags me into the garden to play. It's been three days since I sustained a damned sword injury from the swashbuckling Brat Minor. The words "could you just do" have not interrupted a television programme to send me off on some vital mission or other.

But it's so quiet. I cannot settle. Why, when she is nearly thirty miles away, do I feel so guilty sitting in the armchair? If she looks for evidence of my activities while she has been away I shall have to claim that I have used the period of solitude as thinking time. That I have been planning for the autumn season of "could you just do" jobs.

Behind every successful man, it is said, there is a woman. This is true. I am missing being driven ever onward and there is a severe danger that I might learn the art of relaxation and stay long enough in an armchair for it to assume my shape. I thought it was supposed to feel good when you stopped banging your head against a brick wall, but somehow I miss the pain.

I have also realised that the wallet fairy is also the beer fairy. The remaining can was sunk a couple of nights ago and a further supply has not mysteriously appeared in the cupboard as it usually does. I may live to regret this, but come back Mrs H. I promise that I really will fix the dripping bathroom tap. And I didn't let on about your age.

Oh, by the way dear, we're right out of chocolate biscuits.

FIGURING OUT A NEW WAY TO ARGUE

You must have built up a reasonable impression of me over the last year or so. Pretty decent sort of chap, thinks the world of his wife, works hard to keep the wolves from the Fortress door behind which I shoulder an enormous workload. Tolerant with the Brats. Overall, a kindly sort of soul wouldn't you say?

If you find that an arrogant assessment, just ask Mrs H. Her opinion of me is even better. She accuses me of being too nice. Yes, really, it seems that I am too obliging. Well, to be honest, that is not exactly what she said when she exploded yet again the other day as I was trying to be my usual accommodating self.

"Do you want tea or coffee?" was the question that caused all the fuss.

"I don't mind," I replied helpfully, "whichever is easier." Now I ask you, what could be more considerate than that? It seems that this falls in the category of indecision, not of help.

"I do wish you would make up your mind. You can have what you like, just say. Don't you realise how annoyed people get when you won't say exactly what you want?" I was about to ask who else had complained about my indecisiveness but decided that this was a Mrs H euphemism. She is good at those. If I chance to forget to do something, she will say "Every time I ask you to do something, you always forget." Sometimes I feel she may be exaggerating just a trifle.

Mrs H also finds it unhelpful if I am unable to respond constructively to the question "What would you like for dinner on Sunday?" She does, of course, ask this immediately after she has filled me up with a meal of gargantuan proportions and the last thing I wish to discuss is food. If I do manage to come up with a suggestion, it is always something for which she has not got the ingredients or the Brats won't eat.

As I am clearly such an obliging chap, I have decided to put forward ideas that will further enhance the smooth running of the daily Fortress life. The first issue to target will be any arguments that may arise. I shall be putting my plans to the next full conference of the inmates of Fortress Haverson. It may be necessary to raise the issues at one or two fringe meetings first. It is always useful to have the support of one or both Brats before I start.

The idea is this. All regular areas of friction will be allocated a number. When a situation arises, the appropriate number will simply be shouted out. This dispenses with the necessity to indulge in a full marital battle, in which each of the warring factions knows exactly what the other is going to say.

I suppose it will mean that, in cases where I am being challenged on breaking Fortress rules, then I will also have to allocate a number to my excuses. A typical situation might be when I arrive home late. Instead of giving me the old "Where have you been - do you know what time it is - the children have been in bed for over an hour - Brat Major ate your tea" she will merely shout, with as much venom as she can inject into it, "Number five". It could be also that I have had too much to drink. In which case, she may well feel the need to bellow "and number seven".

For my part, there no longer will be the need to throw in a touch of the "I met old so-and-so and he insisted I have another drink - well you know he hardly ever buys a round - I couldn't turn down a chance like that and I hope Brat Major is sick". Instead, I will bark, or more likely slur in reply, "Numbuzz four 'n nine" and that will be the end of it.

Who am I kidding? At the risk of making an inflammatory comment, women do have a knack of protracting an argument long past its sell-by date. I suspect our contest of marital bingo could well go on.

And if you disagree with that, dear, all I can say to you is, number six.

BREACH OF FORTRESS SECURITY

We are very security conscious at Fortress Haverson. The portcullis has a deadlock and there are locks on all the windows.

It will not surprise you to learn that the Head of Fortress Security is Mrs H. We, the inmates, undergo regular training on keeping the place secure. We have not gone as far as digging a moat round the house but I am sure, given half the chance, Mrs H would invest in a couple of Dobermans to roam freely around the estate. I have thought of the ultimate deterrent. Posting a notice outside which says: "Warning. These premises are patrolled by Mrs H." That should scare 'em off.

In spite of all the strict procedures, I have to report that there was an attempted penetration of Fortress security. Fortunately, thanks to Madam Securicor, the day was saved. You are probably thinking that someone must have tried to break in to steal the family silver. In fact the breach was not due to unwelcome visitors trying to get in but to errant Brats trying to get out.

Enid Blyton has a lot to answer for. Having been totally absorbed in the exploits of the Famous Five and the Secret Seven, the Brats decided that they would create their own adventure featuring the Truculent Two. Brat Major confided the idea to me. I thought it was just a game when she told me that they planned to get up at 1 am and make their way into the village in search of adventure. She implored me not to tell Mrs H, which gives you a clue as to who is seen as a soft touch in the household.

I thought no more of it until the Brats were getting ready for bed. Brat Major has inherited her mother's ability for organising and I overheard her telling her brother that she had got out some warm clothes for him for the adventure and where he would find them hidden.

I still thought that it was in the imagination until I happened to go into Brat Major's bedroom later that evening when she was asleep. I spotted our rucksack, which is normally kept in the spare room, sticking out from under a place where a rucksack should not be. I extracted it from its attempted hidey-hole and discovered that it was bulging with all sorts of things.

Neatly packed was a torch each, a compass, a code book, a

blanket, a game, two cartons of drink, sweets, a blanket, woolly hats, scarves and gloves. There was also a notebook and pencil which I learnt later was to take note of any houses that were being burgled. What they were going to do with this information I do not know. Probably knock those houses off their own list of potential blags.

I was still of the opinion that it was all a game, even though I checked Brat Minor's room and unearthed his winter boots, thick jeans and jumper neatly folded and secreted under his school clothes. Anyway, they hadn't set their alarm clocks so they would never wake up.

Nevertheless, in accordance with Fortress guidelines, I informed the Head of Security. She advised me that, when I had locked both the front and back doors, I should hide all keys. This I did. I remember waking in the night and hearing a bedroom door close but forgot about the adventure until the following morning when the Truculent Two descended upon me with combined wrath to complain that their adventure had been scuppered because they couldn't escape. They said I must have told their mother, who "always spoils our fun".

I pointed out that they are not allowed out on their own during the day let alone at night. Ever since then security has been doubled and Enid Blyton banished to the top shelf until the spirit of adventure dies down.

The trouble is, every time I hear them moving about upstairs, I imagine that they are plotting something. I am sure that next time I go up into the loft I shall find a partly-constructed glider. And that heap of soil on the lawn. Is it really a mole hill or the result of tunnelling Brats?

FEMALES STRIKE BACK
AT LAST

Last Saturday, as I let out the clutch, I realised that my exit from the drive of Fortress Haverson was blocked by the neighbour's car, manoeuvring in the road outside. Then she spotted me. Arms waving she leapt from her vehicle. Something told me that she was trying to communicate so I opened the door.

Dear neighbour informed me that she was just off to purchase her copy of the EDP. Should there be anything too derogatory in my column about Mrs H or the female population in general she would be round forthwith to "beat you up".

I returned to the safety of the car. However, she who had issued the threats of GBH remained stationary. Her car had conked out. Guess who risked hernia, back-strain, even a recurrence of that hamstring injury, to push her stranded chariot back into the drive?

It was with some relief that, while washing the car on Sunday morning, I received communication through the open window across the road that nothing too offensive had been found and that I would survive another week without a bruising.

I do seem to attract these comments. People greet me with such opening lines as, "Is she still living with you?" and "How on earth does your wife put up with you?" I cannot understand this. All I do is set before you my banana skin of a life. In return I receive all this abuse. Surely it is I who should be attracting the sympathy. No-one ever comes up to me and says, "You poor old chap. It must be a terrible life for you and your son with those two women in the house. However do you remain so cheerful."

I am not quite sure how people perceive Mrs. H. Some seem to think that she is a beleaguered mother and housewife, others that she is a nagging harridan. Last Sunday, an incident occurred which gave a limited public insight into my life at Fortress Haverson. I will recount it simply so you can tell where the sympathy should be directed.

I was at the rear of Fortress H where there are a couple of small fruit trees. This is annual hack time, when I render them even smaller. The operation is carried out with a total absence of science or any real understanding of the subject, I simply attack the trees with loppers and pruning saw and have an indiscriminate cull of untidy branches. I must be getting it right as each year they reward us with fruit.

The female inmates were indoors and I was being assisted by Brat Minor. When I say assisted, what he had done was to delve into his junior carpentry kit to find his saw. He then proceeded, with this happily blunt instrument, to attempt to saw a twig, although it looked more as though he was practising for a career in finger amputation.

Meanwhile, I was locked in combat with a particularly obstinate branch.

Except for my sawing, the neighbourhood was quiet. Other husbands were no doubt engaged in more worthwhile pursuits such as reading the Sunday papers or making their way up to the pub. Then the relative peace was shattered. The back door opened and Brat Major sang out, for all the neighbours to hear, "Daddy, you've got to come in now and help get the dinner ready."

It wouldn't have been so bad if it had ended there. I could have made a discreet exit from the tree and slunk indoors. But Mrs H's angry tones followed Brat Major's revelations, making it clear that there had been an attempt to protect my lumberjack image. "Not so loud, I told you to go down the garden and tell him. I could have opened the door and shouted at him." See what I mean? Butling comes before tree surgery. A chap can't even have a quiet prune.

The thing is, I know what she will say in a couple of months; she will peer out of the window and exclaim "Look at those fruit trees. You should have pruned them ages ago. I suppose it won't get done now."

Women's logic. You just can't win. Oh dear, I bet that's set me up for a knee-capping from GBH, the neighbour.

A VOICE WHICH BRINGS US TO HEEL

Mrs H said pointedly the other day, "John has bought Celia a dishwasher."

Clearly I was expected to respond in some way to this statement. No doubt words to the effect of "Here is the cheque book. Off you go and buy yourself one" would have fitted the bill. Instead I opted for the more pious route. You already have a dishwasher my dear," I replied. "You also have a lawnmower, a paint roller, an occasional bath cleaner, not to mention your very own personal alarm clock. All these domestic gadgets come in one cheap and cheerful package called a husband."

Mrs H almost choked on her egg sandwich made, I might add, by none other than the sandwich-maker. "Huh!" she exclaimed, "Do you want me to list all the things I do? And anyway, when was the last time you did anything that you didn't want to do. Nobody ever does what I say. In fact I don't think any of you listen to a word I say."

I know why Mrs H doesn't think I listen to her. She claims that I do not look at her when she is talking to me. I carry on reading the paper or fiddling with something. "Give me your full concentration," she will plead. "Aren't I worth five minutes of your time? Is what I have to say so boring?" Absolutely not, dear. I was riveted by what you and the neighbour (yes that neighbour, GBH) had to say to each other at the school gates.

I think it is all in the voice. As Mrs H spends, as any mother does, long periods of time cajoling the Brats into doing as they are told, it is understandably difficult for her to change the tone of her voice when she wishes to address me. If, for example, she has been giving them a roasting and wishes to say something to me immediately afterwards, I often receive the communication at a higher than necessary number of decibels.

This was brought sharply into focus the other Saturday in an incident that proves that we do listen to her. Perhaps I should say hear rather than listen - as the significance of what has been said does not always register. We were milling around in the kitchen.

This does not go down too well in the first place, as we are invariably under Mrs H's feet as she is trying to perform some culinary feat to enhance the Fortress meal table. In frustration an instruction was issued. Before we realised it, all three of us found ourselves climbing the stairs to "tidy those disgusting bedrooms." Halfway upstairs, I realised that the order was not necessarily aimed at me. However, having got out of the kitchen, it seemed sensible to keep going before alternative employment came my way.

It cannot be easy for mothers who have been chatting with their children to suddenly switch to adult mode. One of Mrs H's chums arrived at Fortress Haverson the other day. Mrs H was out and I answered the door. The lady was with her two little children. As I opened the door, she cocked her head on one side, flashed a sugary smile and sang out, "Hello. Is mummy in?"

As she spoke, she realised what she had said and the way that she had said it. Her face assumed the hue of a setting sun and she began to splutter an apology. "Oh! I am sorry. I do apol... I was expect... I had just been talking to my children." Her embarrassment was total. By the time I had managed to gurgle that mummy had gone shopping, she had babbled out an almost unintelligible message for Mrs H and vanished over the horizon.

I remember one occasion when we were out, Mrs H gave an admiral demonstration of her communication skills. She was fighting a losing battle to persuade a fidgeting Brat Minor to stay still. Finally, in exasperation and for all around to hear, she screamed "Sit!" as loudly as she could.

While this had no effect on Brat Minor, an adjacent Labrador sunk instantly and obediently to his haunches. I know how he felt.

INCREDIBLE SHRINKING
PAIR OF TROUSERS

Now here's a bit of romance to start with this week. I can still remember the first words I spoke to Mrs H. She was coming down some stairs as I arrived at the bottom. Summoning all my skill in the chat-up department, I came out with the gem, "That looks smart".

All right, I know it was hardly original, but I did mean it and it got us into conversation. I was referring to what she was wearing, which was what I called a bright red suit. From that moment, she started as she clearly intended to continue the rest of our relationship, by putting me right. It was, apparently, a cerise suit.

The purpose of re-counting this is that Mrs H had made this suit herself. So the difficulties surrounding a pair of my trousers in the tale I am about to tell were not due to lack of skill of the seamstress. The trousers in question were actually purchased on my behalf by the good lady herself. However, my exact inside leg size was not in stock, so they needed turning up. That was almost two years ago. Said trousers have surfaced on and off over the ensuing period only to disappear again with not even Mrs H being absolutely sure where they were.

Sometimes I would search them out and just finger them, imagining what it might be like to wear them. On long winter nights I would get out the receipt and read it through, just to remind myself that I could in fact claim rightful ownership to them. The receipt has gone now. It is the property of Dairy Crest with "No silver top today, please" written on the back.

Many other things have been submitted to the Fortress sewing surgery during the last two years and been successfully treated with the needle. But for some reason my grey trousers remained on the inoperable list.

Finally, things came to a head last week. The Parent Teachers' Association Christmas bash was looming when Mrs H remarked, "You need a pair of grey trousers to go with your blazer for the PTA do".

I could not let the opportunity pass. I directed my gaze wistfully towards the horizon and mused "Once I had a pair of grey trousers. I wonder what happened to them. Were they in that bundle you sent to Romania?"

She disappeared, returning with the trousers. Firstly they were examined to see if they could still loosely be described as in fashion. They passed that test, so the shortening equipment was extracted from the sewing box. Pins, scissors, needle and thread. She even had the right-coloured cotton. Then the wicked twist was revealed.

I put them on for the pinning up ceremony, only to find that the wretched things fitted perfectly. How could this be? I certainly haven't got longer legs. Had we hit upon something here? Self-shortening trousers? Are your trousers too long? Simply leave them in the dark for two years and watch the material vanish.

So I was all kitted out for the binge. I wasn't too sure about wearing these grey trousers. GBH was going to be there. If any of my blood was spilled, it would show. In the event, there was a minor confrontation on the dance floor. I clung to Mrs H for support but she seemed firmly of the opinion that this was one battle which I should fight solo. After a verbal lashing from GBH, I was allowed to continue dancing, but later another skirmish threatened.

My ability to do the Hokey Cokey and Knees Up Mother Brown after a pint or two is not what it was, so I was not in mint condition when Mrs H informed me that we were walking home with the neighbours. Fortunately, I spent most of the journey chatting to husband of GBH about important issues, such as football and the quality of that night's ale, so I came out of the evening unscathed.

However, I must speak the truth behind one incident which occurred as we neared our respective dwellings. If you live in the vicinity of Fortress Haverson, you may have been woken recently in the early hours of the morning when a soprano voice burst spontaneously into a not altogether tuneful rendition of O Come All Ye Faithful. I'll give you a clue. It wasn't Mrs H.

INCIDENT WITH THE BREAD KNIFE

I have reason to believe that Mrs H has become unstable. I feel obliged to make this public in the interests of any would-be callers at Fortress Haverson.

Small, otherwise inconsequential, things began to happen. As she hung out the washing, she complained bitterly that it was as dirty as when it went in the machine. The washer had, in fact, done its best considering that Mrs H had failed to insert the soap powder.

Talking of the washing machine, it is situated at the same end of the kitchen as the waste bin. I have observed Mrs H on more than one occasion about to fling an empty cereal box or the like into the front loader. Perhaps that explains where my shirts keeping disappearing, too. I'd better check the bin bags before they are collected in future. And I believed her when she said that they were in her mending box to have a button sewn on.

All this could be put down to either an overloaded memory or one simply failing due to the advancing years. But then there came the incident with the bread knife. Mrs H was in the Fortress kitchen. Aided by the microwave and Delia (here's one I put in the oven earlier) Smith, she was creating a gastronomic delight at which the Brats would, no doubt, just a few hours later, be turning up their noses.

She claims that all of a sudden she heard this gentle thud in the hall. The doors were locked and the place was Brat-less at the time. Much as she may have wanted to blame me, I was a good 10 miles away. Coolly, she went to the kitchen drawer, extracted the bread knife and headed for the hall to deal with the intruder. There was no one there. Nor was there any sign of anything that may have gone bump. When I arrived home she gave me a full account of how she stalked the non-existent interloper complete with a demonstration of how she intended to wield the knife.

Suddenly I realised that it could have been me. Suppose I had returned home early clutching a bunch of fresh flowers to surprise my lovely wife. My reward would have been to receive the treatment normally reserved for a crusty farmhouse loaf. I felt moved to share this thought with Mrs H. It wasn't that she agreed with my sentiments that bothered me but the glint in her eye as she mulled over the prospect.

I called a meeting of the other inmates to decide how to handle this. Suppose Mrs H had an attack during the night and went for the bread knife while we were asleep. Or worse still while one of us was making a sleepy visit to the loo in the early hours. There is no telling what lasting damage she might do with one swish of the blade.

Brat Minor immediately issued each one of us with one of his damned swords. He is now teaching me how to get a good night's sleep while clutching the sword in readiness to repel a limb-severing onslaught.

Fortunately reassurance arrived in the form of Mrs H waving one of her women's magazines. "It's all in here," she informed me excitedly. "It's the locus coeruleus." Of course. How stupid of me. The problem was staring me in the face all the time. What on earth was she on about now?

Apparently, the locus coeruleus is an area of the brain thought to be responsible for anxiety and fear. As one gets older there are fewer active brain cells in the locus coeruleus which has a calming effect, making the person more stable and, wait for it, more mellow.

Oh bliss! A mellow Mrs H. Can I look forward to the pipe and slippers era? Will I be coming home to a serene spouse untroubled by rampant Brats and in complete control of a hitherto chaotic Fortress H?

Watch this space.

TIME TO BLOW
MY TRUMPET

Did I talk of a mellow Mrs H last week? No signs yet. Fortress H is still being policed with as much enthusiasm and vigour as ever.

Only this week I was receiving a swift job appraisal from her. However, on this occasion I did strike back. My failure to complete certain items of home maintenance within a specified time scale was being discussed. In fact, I was giving her a damn good listening to. I had failed to deal with peeling paint in the bathroom. The garden, apparently is a mess and, as for Brat Major's bedroom, well: "The poor little thing hasn't had it decorated since she was born."

The Brats think that this is a hoot. I wonder what they tell their mates at school about me. Perhaps their teachers give them extra tuition to make up for having me as a father.

My mind drifted away from the verbal correction I was receiving to ways of bringing out my achievements. "I have an idea," I said soberly. That statement in itself silenced Mrs H. "I am going to purchase a notebook. It will be one of those with an alphabetical index down the side. Each time I get something right, I or any member of the family must enter my achievement in the book."

I brushed aside the hurtful comments about the small number of pages that the book would need to contain, and continued: "This book will be kept in the Fortress hall like a visitor's book. At times like this it will be brought out and extracts read to reassure not only me but my children that I have, on occasions, performed to the required standards."

There are already a number of historical entries that can go in. Under C there will be "car". There was the time I repaired that rust hole. Filled it, rubbed it down, painted it. It's true it started off as a pinprick but by the time I had finished my preparatory work it was about the size of a satsuma.

And under P, what about that plumbing on the pipework that leads to the radiator in the north wing? Leaky joint replaced with the help of my brother's blow-torch. Granted, his flame-thrower was intended for larger jobs. But it didn't take that long to redecorate the wall where the paintwork had been torched. Talking of paintwork, also under P, that happy time when I painted the walls of the front room in our first house just after we were married. The emulsion went on perfectly - both times. As I stepped back to admire my brushwork, I crashed into the ladder on which I had foolishly left a tray of emulsion. As it flipped over, it dispensed its contents all over t he freshly-painted wall. The new Mrs H cried - with laughter, of course.

D will record my Herculean efforts with the drains. On a pitch-black night I ventured out in the driving wind and rain in an attempt to clear the drains which had become blocked at an awkward kink in the pipework. I battled valiantly for some time to remove the stubborn man-hole cover. Having done this, my pathetic prods were ineffective so I scrubbed up and drove 10 miles to borrow a set of rods. The aroma of the journey hung in the car for weeks.

On my return, with the appropriate equipment, I was able to bring relief to the pent-up inmates of Fortress H. A few days later I discovered, hiding beneath a paving slab, another manhole cover immediately over the kinked pipework specifically installed for such emergencies to enable the bend to be unblocked in seconds.

At least I can make an entry under F with confidence. Fatherhood: surely I got that right. There they are, two healthy brats. Perhaps not, though. Having just heard Brat Minor's unofficial version of Mary Had a Little Lamb and been privy to an entry in Brat Major's secret diary, maybe I have failed here too.

I am not sure that this book is such a good idea after all. Mrs H strikes again. See entry under R: "Right - Mrs H always is."

A CASH FLOW
COUNTER ATTACK

Got a financial problem? Is the bank manager asking for his money back and you haven't got the wherewithal? Or, perhaps more to the point, you may have the money but don't wish to part with it.

Try this for size: when your bank manager requests the return of his cash, plus that little bit extra to which he always seems to think he has a right, meet him face to face. Take something with you such as a model of a dinosaur. The species is immaterial, but a large effigy of a Tyrannosaurus is ideal. When he confronts you and demands what is apparently his, hurl the dinosaur on the floor with as much venom as you can muster. Next, scream that it is just not fair and that everyone in the whole wide world is always after your money. Throw yourself to the floor, indulge in a session of uncontrollable hysterics, then rush out of the room making sure you slam the door as hard as you can.

This is the tried and tested method of defaulting on loans, according to Brat Minor. His unwillingness to part with his money goes beyond the point of thrift. This, combined with the state of his bedroom, indicates that he is showing all the signs of become one of those hermits who live in squalor then die leaving a vast fortune hidden under the mattress.

He's a bit of a con artist really. His tactic seems to be to get you in a shop full of customers then put on the wide-eyed innocent little boy act. He looks appealingly at you and says, in a loud voice, that he has set his heart on that particular model of aeroplane. He admits that he has the money to pay for it but, owing to a tragic oversight, has forgotten to bring it with him. If you, his much adored father, could see your way clear to advancing him this small sum he will, of course, reimburse you just as soon as he gets home.

Having been caught by this scam before, I try to resist the loan request, but he always persists. What do you do in front of a shop full of people who are already rooting for him? What a good little boy, they are thinking, and that mean father won't lend him the money. They don't have to deal with the little skinflint when he gets home.

The Fortress Financial Controller, yes that is Mrs H, has tried to instil some responsibility with money into both of the Brats. Mrs H encourages them to put some money by for holidays and save some for spending. Brat Major has all the female attributes in the spending department, but does at least use her own money. Brat Minor, on the other hand, could easily be renamed Brat Miser.

He did splash out on something a while back. He bought himself a lockable cash box. There were two keys, both of which he claims are now lost and this is why, most regrettably, he is unable to pay back his debts.

He seems to know when I am going to ask him for money. He stands defiantly with the dinosaur under one arm and cash box under the other, waiting to go into his routine. Debts going back to last year I have been forced to write off. The tally for this month is a model glider, a key ring and a packet of Maltesers; a total of some £3.75.

After several bouts of dinosaur hurling, he finally agreed to pay me some money and disappeared to his room. After much chinking of coins, he eventually reappeared. He marched up to me and thrust a handful of money at me. "There you are, there's 32 pence. That's all you're getting," he said before stalking off. How he arrived at this arbitrary sum, I know not. I suppose I should be grateful for the gesture, no matter how small.

If, when he gets older, you should chance to meet him in a pub, be warned. Don't buy him a drink.

MY NEW DUTY IS HARD
TO STOMACH

Mrs H sat back in her chair with a sigh of satisfaction and a clean plate in front of her. "Not bad considering I have never had a cooking lesson in my life," she boasted.

Never been taught to cook, huh? That explains a few things. Had I known that all those years ago, as I sank gallantly to my knees, there may well have been few clauses added to the plighting of my troth. I must be honest, Mrs H, self-taught or not, knows her way round the kitchen. She is not afraid to experiment, usually on me. In fact that probably accounts for my complexion.

There were some failures in our early days. The first stab at pastry was a little shaky. In fact a stab was not enough to gain entry to the contents of the pie. It took a sustained period of sawing with a serrated knife to break in.

There were those delicious creme caramels. They tasted superb. The trouble was that they refused to set. I remember suggesting it could be fed to us intravenously. We could have sat watching television hooked to a drip.

Mrs H has gone from strength to strength since those days and we are subject only to the odd blip. Occasionally, some critical ingredient will be accidentally omitted and that which should not crumble does, and the sauce which should be thick and creamy receives a massive injection of cornflour so that it doesn't have to be taken through a straw.

There was quite a scare at Christmas which caused me a bit of stress. Some six hours after making and sampling the icing for the Christmas cake, Mrs H was staggering around Fortress H clutching her stomach complaining of stabbing pains. She became convinced that it was the egg whites in the icing, and that she had inflicted salmonella on herself. Fortunately the icing had not been united with the cake and she came up with the means of testing it to see if it was the cause of her not inconsiderable pain. "You'll have to have a couple of spoonfuls to see if it affects you in the same way." Thanks.

You may think, like me, that it might be better to sacrifice such things as a couple of egg whites and a bowl of icing sugar rather than risk poisoning someone. Not the thrifty Mrs H. It's obviously cheaper to play Russian Roulette with my digestive system.

The following six hours were tense. Every twinge was monitored and discussed to see if I had been successfully poisoned. My stint as official Fortress food taster passed without event and the cause of Mrs H's agony remains a mystery.

I must be honest and say that Fortress H catering is first class but it is not easy providing nourishment for two fickle Brats. What they were eating last week is invariably described as "disgusting" this week. Having consumed Weetabix for breakfast almost since birth, suddenly it makes them feel sick. That usually means that their mates at school are all into Shredded Wheat.

Mrs H and I are very similar in this way and even now we get a bit tense if asked out to dinner. On one occasion the anxiety showed through and Mrs H dropped her guard. We had no idea what our hostess would serve up and by the time the main course arrived on the table we were at fever pitch.

A plate of rice appeared, so far so good. Then a casserole with the lid on so we could not see its contents. The suspense was killing us. The lid was removed. It was a cold sauce and we both breathed in to gain a clue from the aroma. It looked as though it was of a curry ilk. Mrs H was first to take the plunge.

She bravely thrust a forkful into her mouth. "Coo," she explained with relief oozing from every word, "It tastes better than it smells!"

For some reason we were never invited back there again.

RESTLESS NIGHT WITH
EDD THE DUCK

It was a hot day in Bombay. The hostile crows was baying for another wicket. The pitch was taking spin. The wily Indian spinner looped in and bowled a tantalising delivery. I danced gracefully down the track and struck the ball majestically through the covers for another stylish boundary.

Somebody rushed up and patted me on the back. I looked round and discovered it was Mrs H. I also discovered that it was 12.45 in the morning and I had been woken from my reverie by an anxious wife.

Brat Minor was feeling rather seedy and his mother was so concerned that she wanted to keep an eye on him. She was, therefore, in the process of shuffling the sleeping arrangements. He was to move into the master bedroom with her. Even in my sleepy state, I realised that this could mean only one thing. I was to spend the night in Brat Minor's squalid dormitory. I stumbled from bed and made my way to his dimly-lit room. I surveyed my temporary quarters. Watching over me from his chest of drawers was a collection of dinosaurs. Stacked by his bed, ready for action, was a selection of those damned swords, with a new addition to his armoury of a battery laser-powered gun that, when activated, could wake the dead.

Strategically placed to cause maximum damage to a foot should a sharp exit from the bed be called for, was a heap of discarded Lego. And should I be unable to sleep, there were his library books. Nothing from the children's section but two on football and one on modern weaponry.

I slid nervously between the sheets. Fortunately, Mrs H had swapped pillows so I did not have to put my face where that grotty little nose had been. As my feet went down the bed they came in contact with something soft. I never dared look to see what it was. I managed to convince myself it was his Edd the Duck glove puppet. If it wasn't, I felt I'd rather not know.

Secure in the knowledge that I had the means to defend and entertain myself, and was guarded by an assortment of prehistoric monsters, I drifted into slumber to continue my match-winning innings. At 1 am precisely I was, for the second time that night, brought sharply back to consciousness. One of Brat Minor's digital watches was bleeping furiously as programmed by its young owner. I wrestled with various buttons but could not bring a halt to its wretched twittering. My fellow inmates reported the next morning that they all heard me fling open the bedroom door and hurl it downstairs.

Finally I fell asleep but, sadly, was unable to continue my dream. I awoke with a start before the alarm went off. As I sat up in bed, I panicked momentarily as I was confronted with the smirking face of an astronaut. Then I remembered where I was and realised that I was locking eyes with Brat Minor's picture of a grinning Alan Tracy of Thunderbirds fame. I thrust a foot out of bed and trod firmly on the Lego. With a howl of pain I set off to rouse the rest of the household.

After a fitful night's sleep, I was not in the best of moods by the time I reached my rightful bedroom. My humour was not improved to find Brat Minor ensconced in my position in the bed, peering over the duvet with yah boo sucks grin on his face. I cheered up when I learned that Mrs H had slept no better than I. The little heap beside her had snuffled, hacked and wheezed for most of the night. He also cheered up when he learned that he was to have a day off school. However, by the time I returned home in the evening he had been whipped off to the doctor and was on a course of foul-tasting medicine.

Now I have Brat Minor's cold. Unintentionally, I got my own back on Mrs H. It was 12.17 am when, with a violent spasm of coughing, I awoke her as abruptly as she had awakened me a few nights before. She urged me to take something for my throat. I could tell that she was not best pleased at being woken up. Now I wonder what she was dreaming about.

THE DAWN CHORES AT THE FORTRESS

One of those "could you just do" jobs which had matured into an "are you ever going to get round to" nag has finally been crossed off the list. I sacrificed two valuable days' holiday clamped to the end of a paint roller dealing with the peeling paint in the bathroom.

Mrs H claimed that she had reached the stage of being too embarrassed to ask anyone back to Fortress Haverson in case they wanted to use the facilities. She said that she was ashamed to let them view the healthy growth of mould, thriving on its regular diet of condensation. To reduce the moisture, and therefore the mould, the Brats had volunteered to bath less often. Anyone who has had a whiff of Brat Minor by the time Saturday night arrives will understand why this generous gesture was declined.

Usually when I am on holiday the Brats are off school, because I have been instructed to take some leave to "be with your children". I am required to assist in keeping them occupied and generally deter them from driving their mother round the bend.

These two decorating days were taken specifically when they were at school, to allow me to graft away uninterrupted and to eliminate the possibility of little persons knocking over cans of paint and relocating the contents to all parts of Fortress H by means of their feet. This meant that I was able to share in that joyous ritual of getting the children ready for school. Usually I have left for work at about the time the Brats have been washed and fed, but what happens after I have left defies belief. It seems that the nearer the time to leave for school approaches, the more the situation deteriorates.

As I attacked the paintwork, Mrs H attacked the Brats. Well, verbally anyway. The path is so well trod that timings are down to perfection. In other words, Mrs H can tell exactly how late for school each of them will be. It is the last five minutes where the battle is lost. Mrs H's words of encouragement and the response of the Brats are also well-used. To such an extent that Mrs H answers the moans and whinges before they are voiced.

"Put your coats on - and do them up. Yes, you will need them done up; it is freezing out there. And yes that does mean we are walking, not going in the car. No that doesn't mean you can take that damned sword with you. I'm not carrying it all the way home."

On the first morning I rolled the paint on the walls listening to Mrs H's well-rehearsed routine. Had I not been there, I would not have believed that anything up to half an hou r could pass without either Brat making any progress towards being ready for school.

The next day I was invited by Mrs H to delay my start on the painting to see if I could hurry them along. "You'll have to keep behind them," she insisted. "One will disappear and start reading her library book and the other will recreate world war two with his aeroplanes." I patrolled the table as they shovelled down their breakfast. I supervised the activities in the bathroom, making sure that Brat Minor brought the soap in contact with the many neglected parts of his unsavoury little body.

I helped him do up his cuffs, which he complains always delay him, and threatened to cut short Brat Major's hair, there and then, if she did not brush it properly. Like a well-oiled military machine, I put them through their routines and marched them to the front door to a waiting Mrs H.

Then it happened. Brat Major suddenly remembered that she had to take 12 straws and two elastic bands to make a musical instrument. Meanwhile, Brat Minor produced from his school bag a couple of "Dear Parent" letters that should have been signed and returned the day before.

We were well into injury time by the time Mrs H threw open the door and began to usher them out. I hardly dared mention it. "Excuse me," I piped up hesitantly. "Does he always go to school in his slippers?"

INSPIRED BY A WRETCHED SPONGE

You would not think it possible to find a gardening programme on television particularly contentious. Question Time possibly, but not a half hour on the soil. Well, maybe if you lived at Fortress Haverson and were charged with the task of keeping the estate neat and tidy, you would.

We are situated on clay and, in spite of my efforts to lighten the soil, a good dig is a fork-bending exercise. I feel quite guilty when I insert a few unfortunate parsnip seeds into the stodge knowing that I have sentenced them to struggle like spawning salmon.

After a hernia-inducing session on the Fortress vegetable patch last week, I entered the house with creaking limbs. Such was the effect that I decided to request an increase in my weekly hot water allowance so I could have a soothing bath. It's a good job there is not a severe drought. I was able to ignore the Fortress summer maxim of "Save water, bath with a Brat".

Why am I telling you all this? Simply that this particular wallow inspired my resolve to stand up for myself and the younger inmates against all things trivial that can turn an otherwise rational human being into a snarling brute. You know the sort of things. There's always someone who never replaces the loo roll when it runs out.

So why should a bath bring out the worst in me? It is all due to the sponge. All we inmates know that it is incumbent upon the bather to ensure that there is no tidemark left round the bath after we have let out the water. To assist us in this Mrs H has kindly left a sponge for removing, in my case, the residue of the clay. Insisting that there is nowhere else for it, Mrs H always leaves it wedged by the cold tap, and that is what causes us the hassle. What invariably happens occurred yet again last week and I thought, enough is enough.

I had put in the plug, pinched some of Brat Minor's Swamp Monster Magic Colour Change Bubble Bath and turned on the hot tap. After a short spell I turned on the cold tap. As usual my hand caught the wretched sponge and it plunged eagerly into my hot foaming bath. With a screech of exasperation, I thrust in a hand to retrieve it. With a howl of pain, I withdrew my scalded hand rapidly, clutching the damn thing. Incensed and semi-naked, I stormed out of the bathroom to confront a bewildered family with the sponge dripping from a somewhat red hand.

"It's happened again" I yelled. "Can't you find somewhere else for that damned sponge? Either that or I am taking my last ever bath." With that little outburst I turned on my heel and, pausing only to stub my toe on the door jamb, I left the rest of them stunned as I returned to the bathroom, defiantly abandoning the sponge on the window sill. As I languished in the tub, I thought of all the other irritating things I could get my teeth into. Ah! The bread bin, that's next. We have a breadbin with a flat top on the kitchen work surface. This provides a convenient dumping point for such things as letters and unpaid bills.

Over the years this small area has taken on the role of in tray, out tray, and pending, to such an extent that Mrs H even keeps a diary on it. It is such a bind to move all this lot that I always try to prise the bread out of the container without disturbing Mrs H's office. Of course, I rarely succeed and the whole lot usually ends up all over the place. British Telecom take note. That is why, when the Fortress phone bill is paid, it is usually served in breadcrumbs.

With the initiation of my new campaign to eradicate the irritating, I resolved to leave all the bits and pieces where they ended up, should they choose to cascade everywhere.

I am sure I will find other things against which I will take a stand. All I can say is, thank goodness I haven't got any annoying habits.

TWO'S TROUBLE ON A
FOETAL PHONE

I was interested to read in the papers this week, of the three year old boy who has the reading ability of a six year old. He can do useful things like recite the Greek alphabet and count in three languages. This advanced ability is put down to the fact that his parents read and talked to him while he was still in the womb. Doctors say that, during the final weeks of pregnancy, the baby can hear accurately. Sound is transmitted via the amniotic fluid.

I do not believe that this is anything new. It is just that adults have not been aware of it.

I am convinced that the recently-born can communicate with the unborn. When Brat Minor joined the payroll, Brat Major was two years old. What we experienced, as have countless other parents, were not spontaneous demonstrations of mischief, but carefully-laid plans orchestrated to cause maximum parental stress and havoc.

I have little doubt that, during Mrs H's pregnancy, Brat Major was constantly on the foetal hotline briefing her unborn brother on our weak spots and how most to exploit them. Lengthy explanations about "Mummy's bump" provided ample opportunity for her to get on the umbilical cordless 'phone and practise her toddler telepathy. They gave us two weeks to settle into a routine before they decided that we were ripe. We were softened up with the alternate waking routine throughout the night. How each knew when it was his or her turn to wake up remains a mystery, but their timing was impeccable.

We would just get one settled down and be tumbling over the precipice of sleep when a desperate howl from the other room would have us dragging ourselves out of bed again. After a few nights of this we were red-eyed and totally dancing to their tune.

Nappy-changing gave them their best sport with us. The opportunities to stretch our already overstrained patience were endless.

To give ourselves a fighting chance we would, if possible, work together to perform what would have been an otherwise simple operation. Firstly we would open the baby box containing all the necessary equipment. This box turned out to be an Aladdin's cave for Brat Major. Once all the gear was ready, tops of jars off cream etc., it was not just the baby's bottom that was exposed. We were defenceless. Kicking over a bowl of water to distract our attention, dear daughter ghosted in on the blind side and scooped up a handful of zinc and castor oil cream with a skill that augured well for a career in a fast food chain.

Neatly side-stepping a lunge from her mother, something I have been trying to perfect for years, she set about her task of daubing cream on as many pieces of furniture as possible before being captured. Finally we would corner her behind an armchair, only to find her grinning contentedly. We had, of course, forgotten about the other little warrior.

Back at battle HQ on the changing mat, he was doing what only baby boys can do successfully, systematically spraying clean vest, Baby-Gro and anything else within infantile range.

Brat Major was the brains behind this and we tried everything from exclusion zones to carrying out the ultimate threat of withdrawal of the chocolate supply. Nothing worked.

I lost count of the number of times that I injected myself with goodness knows what with a nappy pin while fending off a lightning raid.

Take heed, expectant mums. When you are doing your breathing exercises, try a little foetal programming at the same time.

SITTING WITH A STRANGE FAMILY

We inmates of Fortress Haverson are on a strictly-controlled healthy diet. Otherwise, I would say that Mrs H is eating food with too many E numbers in it and is hyperactive. She has to find something to do. The trouble is, I feel obliged to keep going as well.

Unfortunately, Mrs H has passed the itchy feet syndrome on to our daughter. Brat Major is five and a half stone of perpetual motion. She is on the go all the time. Even watching television she is not still. She bounces around on the sofa, doing handstands and performing somersaults. This isn't so bad at home. It is when we go out that it becomes a trifle irritating. We were having a coffee in a well-known department store in Norwich the other Saturday. Brat Major was consuming some sort of tooth-rotting snack while jiggling and fidgeting in her chair. She constantly adjusted her hairband while casting furtive glances around the restaurant.

She then blessed us with one of those moments when a parent wishes passionately that a large abyss will magically appear, down which they may thankfully plunge.

"Look Mummy," she announced through a mouthful of cake, "You can see that lady's bra." She supported her observation by pointing a crumb-festooned finger in the direction of the poor female. While those around us who had picked up this newsflash craned their necks for a glimpse of what they assumed must be a half-naked woman, Mrs H hissed a giggling instruction to her daughter to shut up. I buried my head in my cup of coffee and pretended that it was only through force of circumstance that I was sharing a table with this strange family. Little did I know that my turn for abyss-wishing was to come, courtesy of Brat Minor.

Any sensible parent of young children embarking on an outing will make sure that their offspring have been to the loo before they depart. Once out it is, of course, always prudent to take advantage of a toilet if one is handy to ensure that they go again. We have all been caught out halfway round somewhere like Blickling Hall when the little voice pipes up in the Chinese Room:

"I need to go to the toilet".

So, having waited for the woman with the exposed bra to make good her escape, we too slipped out of the restaurant. As Mrs H had in store for us an intense programme of wallet emptying around the shops, we erred on the side of caution and propelled both Brats in the general direction of the loo, despite their insistence that they did not need to go. Brat Minor and I entered a packed but silent Gents. Because of his lack of height, Brat Minor was unable to point to the porcelain so he grudgingly made for one of the cubicles. After a few seconds the silence was shattered by his piercing voice.

"I can't go. I told you I didn't want to go. I'm not going to do anything." he announced. The rest of the assembled populace began shooting sidelong glances at each other to see who would admit ownership of the inhabitant of the cubicle. Foolishly I tried to bluff my way out of it by keeping my head down and remaining silent. But Brat Minor had a point to make and persisted.

"Dad? Dad? Are you still there Dad?" There was much foot-shuffling going on now. No one seemed to be leaving the toilet. It was as if everybody was hanging on to see, if you will pardon the expression, who would come out of the closet and admit to being the father.

I gave in and all eyes focused on me as I came out with a lame "just do your best". As Brat Minor emerged from the sanctuary of his cubicle, the entertainment continued. Our captive audience was treated to the spectacle of me trying to explain to him why he needed to wash his hands even though he hadn't done anything, and what would happen to him if he dared to say he wanted to go to the toilet when we were half-way up St. Stephen's.

LET'S TALK ABOUT
SEX MUMMY

Mrs H has risen yet further in my estimation. As you will already have gleaned, the esteem in which I hold her is well above rooftop level. But last week her handling of an incident with Brat Major left me speechless with admiration.

Brat Major is well into what might well be referred to as her "curiosity phase". This is that period in a child's life when they have left the protection of the nest and are enjoying all the benefits of mixing with other children who have older brothers and sisters. These streetwise elders are only too happy to pass on to their juniors their worldly knowledge on such matters as procreation and the like. The juniors in turn receive the information but do not understand it. Since their siblings probably do not understand it either, what do they do? Ask their parents, of course.

You can always tell what's coming. There's a certain drawn out inflexion in the way they say "Mu ... mmy." They then deliver a pointed question which leaves the parent scrambling around for an answer that will satisfy the enquiring mind whilst not tarnishing the innocence.

Mrs H had been acquainted with the fact that Brat Major was on the hunt for knowledge while on the way to school one day. Out of the blue, and in a street filled with parents and offspring hurrying to school, she bluntly asked, "Mu ... mmy, what's sex?" Passing pupils heading for the adjacent high school, paused, eager to see if their own understanding of the function could benefit from an update by Mrs H. Or was it the other way round? Were they lingering to see if Mrs H needed any help?

Mrs H shifted smoothly into overdrive. Brat Major found her approach to school gathering pace as she was towed rapidly towards the gates. "I don't think this is the place to discuss that," said Mrs H as calmly as the speed at which she was travelling would allow her.

Brat Minor is now into this phase; which reminds me I must fix the lock on the bathroom door. If he happens to catch me in the bathroom when he is in one of his inquisitive moods I can guarantee that a searching question is in the offing. The trouble is, he is so persistent. After I have given the potted biology lesson he will come back with something like, "Yes but Daddy, what are they actually for?"

A contemptuous remark on the subject from Brat Major made me think that Mrs H had answered that question so discreetly posed in the street. I stumbled across Brat Major performing a lightning raid on the fridge. The radio was blaring out as she emerged guiltily from the fridge clutching a carton of orange juice. She jerked her head in the direction of the radio. "You won't want to listen to that," she said disdainfully. "They're talking about sex." With that, she swept out of the room.

Fortunately, the next time she embarked on a quest for information was at home. I was walking down the hall to the kitchen. I was not in sight of Mrs H and Brat Major who were already in the room, when I heard the tell-tale "Mu ... mmy." I stopped dead in my tracks as Brat Major asked the meaning of something which had not been clear to me until long after the back of the bicycle shed era. You're on your own with his one dear, I thought to myself as I waited in the wing to hear how Mrs H would deal with it.

She excelled herself. There was a momentary pause then an explanation which gave the facts without giving away too much background detail. At first I was impressed then a mite puzzled at the extent of Mrs H's knowledge. I really must vet those women's magazines she buys.

Brat Major, meanwhile, was totally satisfied with her answer and hasn't mentioned it since. I did once but Mrs H suddenly developed a headache.

CRANIUM CAUSES
HILARITY

I have a message for my hairdresser - it's not your fault. The comment made by Mrs H in the pub the other night, in front of witnesses, was not aimed at you. It must be my fault for lack of the correct maintenance.

There were four of us putting the world to rights, having attended the annual general meeting of the Middle School Governors. I was the only male. I was quietly indulging in an extremely welcome pint while the three females exchanged notes on their respective Brats. Suddenly I became aware that I was involved in the conversation, as Mrs H swung threateningly in my direction and began to solicit my support for one of her assertions. I was just draining my glass as her critical eyes settled on me. She changed the subject in mid-sentence.

"We were going to weren't we Neil ... Your hair looks awful! It's all flat." This was a conversation-stopper if there was one. I sat there speechless while our friends, Mrs B and Mrs E, hooted with laughter. If I had been told I had spilt beer on my trousers I could have had a look but, sitting there in the subdued lighting of the pub with half the bar taking a raincheck on my hairstyle, which I could not see, was unsettling.

It took a little while for me to take in the logic of this astute observation. As my head, thankfully, is fairly flat, it seems reasonable that my hair, which does after all follow the contours of my scalp, should also be flat. Had I been born with some sort of corrugated head I could have understood the shock. What is more, we had been together all night. How come this startling observation did not come to light until so late? Why did she let me appear in public among all the bouncy, wavy coiffures if I was going to stand out like Kojak in a barber's shop?

I spent the rest of the time in the pub with my head bowed. How can a chap look fellow drinkers in the eye with a flat head of hair? Luckily, Mrs E went to the bar to get the next round so I did not have to expose my hilarious cranium to the rest of the pub. While there, she took the opportunity to wave a glass at the landlord and castigate him on the quality of his washing-up. This deflected the attention away from me.

It cannot be the crimper because we both go to the same place. It has to be the standard of maintenance. My method is to dunk it well, lather it until there is plenty of frothy shampoo not only in my hair but also a liberal covering all over the bathroom - that is something else that annoys her. Repeat the treatment then allow to dry naturally.   Oh, and do not forget to remove any loose hair from the plughole - Mrs H gets really uptight when she next uses the sink and the water will not run away.

When we got home from the pub, I decided to invite constructive criticism on the way I deal with my hair. "You ought to use the hairdryer," advised Mrs H. "It needs to have a bit of body. Perhaps you should try some of my conditioner." I am definitely not getting into the kind of routine that she does just to unflatten my hair. "Now, if I wash it tomorrow, it will need doing again before Saturday." Then I am called in for an opinion. "Do you think my hair looks all right? If I can make it go another day I can wash it on Friday then it will look nice on Saturday night."

To make it "go" an extra day she heats up some evil-looking spiky wand with which she proceeds to coil up her hair. Surely that must do more harm than my low-key approach? And as for washing it, that blasts a hole in the evening. First there is the shampooing of it. Then the application of the conditioner. Once that has been rinsed off, the ritual of the setting of the hair takes place. This is accompanied by a series of curses as rollers are dropped on the floor and those little pin-like things which hold them in place are buried into tender parts of the fingers. Finally the dryer is switched on, rendering conversation impossible and drowning out the television.

If that is what it takes to give it body, I'll stay flat.

THE PAIN WHICH MADE
MY WEEKEND

I led an almost Utopian existence for a few hours earlier this week. A mellow Mrs H contributed to my living the life of Riley on Sunday and Monday. It all came about through a mysterious injury to my shoulder.

I woke up on Sunday morning with severe pain in my right shoulder. How it came about, I just cannot think. The best diagnosis to date was of a Norfolk variety from a colleague at work, "Yew must hev slept funny." This could indeed have been true. I cast my mind back to Saturday to try and recall if I had done anything out of the ordinary which might have caused me to have a bad night or to have strained my shoulder.

The day itself had been a normal Saturday. Mrs H fleeced my wallet and dashed off to the city to see how much hard-earned cash she could shed in the longest possible time. Brat Major went with her leaving me to fend off constant requests from Brat Minor to play cricket with him.

I then attached myself to a variety of gardening implements, such as the lawnmower, a fork and a pair of shears. By the time Mrs H returned to carry out a routine inspection of my achievements, the Fortress garden was looking quite well groomed, and there was every chance that I might be given time off for good behaviour on Sunday. More to the point, I was aware of no strange sensations in my right shoulder.

That evening, we attended the middle school PTA's barbecue. Thanks to the bar, the right arm got its fair share of usage. Even so, I can think of only one thing that could have caused me to sleep "funny". The bitter ran out during the evening and I went on drinking some gassy fluid that I understand is called lager. If there is one thing the Haverson taste buds appreciate, it is a traditional bitter, so after a couple of pints of pop, the old system began to register its disapproval.

Nothing else untoward happened. GBH was there but did not inflict any physical damage on me. Our two families walked home together and there was no attempt to exact retribution, though

GBH threatened to sing when we got nearer home. Fortunately there was an overwhelming majority against an impromptu performance and she remained silent. Well, as quiet as GBH ever is.

I suffered absolutely no ill effects from the fizzy drink the following morning other than the damaged shoulder. I arose gingerly from bed to find that movement of my right arm was severely restricted, not to say somewhat painful. If you are right-handed, it is not easy shaving with your left hand, and manhandling a brat was quite out of the question.

Fortunately, this was kept to a minimum as, on returning from the barbecue, we had temporarily traded a brat for the night. Brat Major went to sleep with Grievous Major while we played host to Grievous Minor. This meant that on Sunday morning Brat Minor had someone to argue with other than me, over the leg-before-wicket law.

Mrs H showed a softer side when she saw my evident agony. I did try to continue with the gardening but anyone in the vicinity of Fortress Haverson would have heard the shriek of pain when I plunged the fork into the soil and my shoulder objected violently. I was taken off fatigues although, with face contorted in pain, I did show willing by helping with the washing-up. Then Mrs H actually encouraged me to take it easy. She used words hitherto unheard within the confines of Fortress H.

"Go and sit down and rest your arm. Read the paper for a little while." Was this all a dream? Things got better. My evening work period was cancelled and I was even coerced into having "a nice hot bath" for reasons other than bodily cleanliness.

By Tuesday night, the pain was easing and my bloodcurdling howls when using my right arm were less convincing. My vast input to the running of Fortress Haverson was clearly being missed and Mrs H started prefixing standard orders with, "If it doesn't hurt your arm too much, could you just ....?"

So the honeymoon was over and normal service was resumed. I enjoyed it while it lasted. I may even take up drinking lager.

HAVING A HOLIDAY
UNDER A CLOUD

The brochure said it was at the foot of the Cheviots. We peered through the window of our remote holiday cottage in the direction of said hills but we couldn't see them. They were being jealously guarded by a protective swathe of heavy, low cloud.

You'll be all right, we were told. The rains tops at the Pennines. You should be dry in Northumberland. Unfortunately, nobody had told the clouds where to stop and they rolled on, dumping their contents on us as if each was on some kind of bonus if it could finish the drought.

With the weather determined to put the dampers on outdoor activities, we took to the stately homes. One of them, we learned, has a very sensitive security system. We joined the throng of other visitors in the great hall of this particular ancient pile. Suddenly a high-pitched alarm began to shriek. You've guessed it. Using all his inherited skill as a clumsy Haverson, Brat Minor had staggered within snatching distance of the family silver. I tried to disown him but, in his panic, he headed straight for his father. This had the effect of bringing expressions of relief to all the other parents in the room who were just thankful it wasn't their offspring upon whom the hidden camera was focused.

Enthused by the weapons he saw at these places, Brat Minor invested in an extension to his armoury. As well as that damned sword and that wretched water pistol, he now has a lethal bow and arrow. This became his constant companion throughout the week. He ate with it, slept with it, he even took it to the toilet. He acquired a quite remarkable accuracy too.

He and I were waiting in the car, one morning, for Mrs H and Brat Major to complete one of those interminable visits to the loo that females make. Also sheltering from the rain was a particularly annoying fly. Suddenly I heard a twang, followed almost immediately by a thwack and then silence. Nonchalantly the young archer peeled his suction arrow from the nearside rear window to reveal a spread-eagled fly whose buzzing days were over.

One other thing for which this particular holiday will be a milestone was the sleeping arrangements. Ever since we have been married, in fact I have ceased to believe that I was single, Mrs H and I have shared a bed. The cottage had twin beds only. These beds were of modern design and pushing them together was hopeless. Any attempt to make a good boarding of the adjacent bed meant a strong possibility of disappearing down a void, damaging something vital on a solid pine frame.

There have been close calls to ending up in separate beds in the past. There are times when matters Fortress are not always as harmonious as they could be. Blame, on these occasions, is always apportioned to me as Mrs H disappears out of the master bedroom door dragging behind her a spare duvet in search of alternative sleeping accommodation. Owing to my masterful diplomacy, we have always woken up in the same bed in the morning.

The other occasion was just two days into our married life, when we were on a touring honeymoon in the south of England. A bed and breakfast landlady ushered us into a twin-bedded room. Mrs H and I exchanged glances. Clearly, in my new role as husband, I was expected to assert myself and remedy the situation.

"We'd prefer a double bed, if you have one," I stammered. Then, to support my case, I added: "You see, we're on honeymoon". The woman snorted. "Huh, Thought you'd prefer to be at the back of the house away from the traffic" she explained as she led a red-faced couple to the double-bedded room.

Once the door was shut, I received what was to become a regular feature of our marriage. It was the chastening "did you have to ..." rebuke.

"Did you have to tell her we were on honeymoon? How do you think I am going to feel when we go down to breakfast?" Hungry, I hoped, but even at that early stage of our union I had already learned that some things are better unsaid.

WHAT A DIFFERENCE
THE YEARS MAKE

If there are four words I dread more than "could you just do ...", I think they must be "I was wondering if ...". The net result is the same but the latter is much softer and usually means that I am being buttered-up for something even more awful than usual.

Last Sunday, Mrs H turned on the mellow tone and with that endearing, sinister smile, issued an "I was wondering if ...". She sells children's books through party plan and was off to a gathering of fellow organisers. To break the ice, the supervisor had decided to kick off the meeting with a light-hearted game. Each organiser had to take along a picture of themselves as a baby and a description of themselves in no more than about 100 words. They had to work out who was whom from the description, then match the photo with the person.

I ask you, can you imagine any woman being able to describe anything in 100 words, let alone themselves? You know what they are like. Never use 10 words when 30 will do. "I don't think I'm that fat. In fact, if I shop at Marks' I can sometimes get into a 12. Do you know, when we were on holiday last year, I tried on this two-piece ..." off they go into overdrive.

Anyway, Mrs H turned to me for assistance, figuring that perhaps I was in the best position to describe her. It was rather like being asked how you want to die, but I thought I would give it a go. Having come up with a couple of paragraphs, I know how Salman Rushdie feels. In the end, we decided to do it together.

Mrs H started with "I was born at Thetford, where I went to school." My opening gambit was "I talk a lot except in the morning when I maintain a stony silence punctuated by the odd Neanderthal grunt"

"That's no good, " she said. "How will anyone else know that?"

Undaunted, Mrs H went on to describe how she took a job in Norwich where she met her husband. They produced two Brats and are now questioning the wisdom of entering the stressful world of procreation. I intervened here with several glowing adjectives describing the husband, but they were deleted as being irrelevant, not to say vain.

"Are you going to mention your thighs?" I asked, bravely. "Or will that make it a dead give-away?" Surprisingly, she seized on this as a positive point. She wrote, "I was 10 stone when I got married but, thanks to regular tap and keep-fit classes, not to mention two active Brats, I am much slimmer now."

There was just the thorny subject of her age to mention. To get round this, we came up with some long-forgotten event in history that took place the same year as she was born. No, I am not even going to give you a clue.

Between us, finally, we painted a picture of some Greek goddess, from which the others were supposed to recognise her. The only thing left to find was a suitable picture of the infant Mrs H. I volunteered to search the archives but rather wished I hadn't. While I emitted several low whistles at the attractive young lady with the hair down to her waist, that I eventually married, I was horrified at the sight of the slim young man without a grey hair on his head that was standing beside her.

At last, I found a picture of a sweet little two-year-old girl that would fit the bill for Mrs H. In the event, no-one recognised her from either the description or the photograph and this caused great celebrations at Fortress H. For Mrs H, this was confirmation that the lifelong battle against the jodhpur thighs has been finally won.

ENCOUNTER WITH A
PACKET OF PEAS

I was woken up last Sunday morning by a packet of frozen peas. This is unusual, even at Fortress Haverson. At first, I thought I was dreaming. Was that gently crunching noise the sound of me dashing through autumn leaves in a desperate attempt to escape from GBH?

However, once my eyes finally opened and began transmitting live pictures to my brain, I realised that Mrs H was clutching a small packet of frozen peas which she was applying gingerly to her forehead. She had a belter of a headache which she readily admits was self - inflicted. Against our better judgement we had been to a 70s disco in the village the previous evening. I say against our better judgement because, if there is one single thing upon which Mrs H and I are in total agreement, it is 70s music. Of the last three decades the 70s are, musically, in our opinion, lucky to make third place.

Firstly we offered to buy tickets, providing there was no obligation to actually go. Then we fell back on the hope that the Brat Warden would be unavailable to baby-sit. This too failed, so as it was for the good cause of raising money for play equipment for the village, we gritted our teeth and went.

The old enemy from across the road, GBH, was also going. We walked there with her goodself and the Gaffer. We walked home together too. Well, he and I did. GBH and Mrs H weaved their own way home a good couple of staggers behind us.

The music was already beating out when we arrived. I say beating, but there seems to be something about the beat of 70s music that makes it difficult for dancing. And I need all the help I can get. Mrs H maintains that I can't dance. She says I don't move from the hips. I practised hard in the bathroom before we left, but there appeared to be no improvement when I gave a live performance to one of those all-time groans, Donny Osmond singing Puppy Love.

It was a good night and the music was quite good too. I only recall one record by that awful Rod Stewart. He has a voice that sounds like someone at a lathe with a blunt chisel, struggling to turn a particularly knotty piece of wood. I think there were a couple of good old stomping numbers from Slade. They certainly placed minimum demands on the English language when they burned the midnight oil writing their lyrics.

I was involved in a couple of incidents that I would otherwise deny. However, there is incriminating evidence. That troublesome Mrs E did a Jeremy Beadle. She kept manifesting herself in all sorts of places clutching a video camera. I have a suspicion that she was getting her own back to previous mentions in this column. First she shot footage of me drinking, but worse was to follow.

I danced with both Beadle and GBH. While I danced with one, the other was busy filming the encounter. Both the dances were slow ones so widespread knowledge of my inability to move from the hips has been contained. Details of initial reactions to Beadle's first showing of the film are filtering back. I may not be alone in offering vast sums to secure exclusive rights.

Mrs H thought all this a great hoot, but I had the last laugh. She claims not to have had time to eat during the day of the disco, owing to the demands placed on her by home and Brat. Hence the meagre amount of alcohol which she drank went to her head.

"Did I do anything embarrassing last night?" she asked when she regained the power of speech. I just sucked my breath in sharply through my teeth with a sad shake of the head. I could have some sport with this one later.

Her condition left her nonplussed about food on Sunday. You will be reassured to know that my appetite was unaffected. Except, I just didn't fancy frozen peas for Sunday lunch.

THE LONG AND SHORT
OF IT IS...

Mrs H and I had this argument the other day. No, seriously, we did. Yes, I know you have this impression that we go through life as a cohesive team, but that's easily achieved. The answer is simply this. We always do what Mrs H wants to do unless it coincides with what I want to do. Then we do just what I want to do. Get it?

Our argument came about as we were off out one night. Mrs H was getting ready, and summoned me for the standard "how do I look?" interview but, on this occasion, I was asked to offer an opinion on the hemline. And what was worse, it was a loaded question to boot. "How does this skirt look?" I was about to select one of the platitudes that I had not used for a while when the twist in the tail was delivered. "You don't think it's too short for someone my age?"

One thing about experience is that you have the support of a little voice which says, "Careful old lad - that was a thorny one." The trouble is, you can't afford to pause while you marshal your thoughts. The slightest hesitation is interpreted as a negative, so the best thing is to throw in a holding question such as an almost indignant "Whatever makes you ask that?"

I did precisely this while searching for the answer that would sound the most plausible and sincere. Where short skirts are concerned my experience tells me that, from the male perspective, they fall into two categories - those that other women wear and those that your own wife or girlfriend wears.

In the first case, the judgement is made entirely on the quality of the leg; the age of the wearer comes a good second. With our own wife, it is closer to home and the hemline has to be well below see-level.

I studied the amount of visible flesh above Mrs H's knee and pronounced it within the bounds of decency. As usual, my opinion did nothing to reassure her so I suggested that we use the evening as a kind of test. As we walked into the room, I would cast my eyes around to judge the reaction of the women. You know what I mean. When a woman enters the arena, it's like parading on the catwalk. Their heads all go together and they whisper something which falls into one of two schools. Either it's "Whatever has she got on tonight - and at her age too. " Or it's "I hate her. If only I had the shape to get away with wearing something like that."

In the end, she had two fellow females actually come up and compliment her on the outfit. I felt this vindicated my opinion and perhaps my view will in future attract more credence than it has in the last 20 or so years. Somehow I doubt it.

The debate on age finally came about a couple of weeks ago when I spied a well-known actor on television. I cannot help watching him with a slight feeling of gloom and I expressed my depression to Mrs H. "Just look at him," I exclaimed, "I am the same age as him. I don't look that old, do I? I know he is a reformed alcoholic which I am not - not an alcoholic I mean, not one that has yet to reform. But I have got you lot to accelerate the ageing process."

I was looking for reassurance here. Something like an expression of utter astonishment that I was anywhere near the age of the person on the screen would have sufficed. The response was, however, rather non-committal. "I don't look at people and wonder how old they are. I look to see what sort of person they are." I thought it better not to pursue that one.

Before I knew it, we had embarked on an argument on when a person actually hits middle age. I maintained that, logically, it must be at about the age of 35 if you take the three-score years and 10 maxim. Mrs H, for reasons that you can easily work out, puts a counter-argument that it in fact starts much later than that.

Don't worry dear, I'll let you know when you get there. I think it's when you are too old to wear short skirts.

YOUNGER DUDES
JUST GROSS!

The Brats were having tea the other night when I arrived home from work. "Hello children, had good day?" I greeted them. Brat Major, who is a committed eater, paid me the compliment of pausing between mouthfuls to answer.

"Yo dude" came her laid back reply. Now, I must admit that I had not been expecting a protracted response such as "Hello father. How was your day? I trust you had a happy and fulfilling time at the office?" But I did expect a bit more than that.

On investigation, I learned that this is economical modern parlance designed to embrace all aspects usually covered by a greeting.

Brat Minor who, when it comes to eating, is in the opposite camp to his sister, simply used my arrival to renew his whinging about having to eat food he claims he does not like.

However, food did come to mind when I invited him to play football at the weekend. Instead of "Gosh dad, what a spiffing idea," he replied simply "Megabrill!" This is an expression of approval but it sounded more like something that McDonalds serve with fries and a touch of relish.

They use initials at school these days. Brat Major has CDT. That stands for craft, design and technology. The nearest we ever got to that was woodwork. And, the other day, Brat Minor announced: "I made an aeroplane in Eric time." "You what?" exclaimed Mrs H, "You know you're not allowed to do that in Eric time." It transpires that Eric time stands for Everybody Reads in Class. Either the Brats read to the teacher or she reads to them. Sometimes the Brat Controller herself will read them a story.

The language of today has buzz words that sound like a foreign tongue. Having said that, I suppose that the inspeak we used years ago was as alien to our parents as the gobbledegook our children use today. The in-word for Brat Major at the moment is "gross." Everything that does not meet her exacting standards is gross. Mrs H's cooking is gross. The other night, as we were getting ready to go out, Mrs H asked her daughter what she thought of the chosen outfit. Answer? "Gross."

I'm having trouble keeping up with all this modern jargon. I've lost all track of the pop groups. In fact I am assured by younger colleagues that they are no longer referred to as groups, they are bands. I ask you, how can you call a guitarist and a harmonica player a band? And you really are a wrinkly if you refer to your favourite group's latest LP. They're called albums now.

My inability to travel from the back door to the shed and retain the reason for my journey highlights how the memory fades. Brats have no such problems. Particularly when it comes to that money you borrowed from their piggy bank because you hadn't got any change when that nice lady called for the Help the Aged envelope.

There are occasions when their memories let them down. Brat Minor forgot himself last week and made it apparent that they use one form of the English language as taught them at home and one as gleaned from the playground.

I had just parked and we were hastening cross the car park. I was leading with Brat Minor, as usual, several paces behind. Suddenly he informed me and anybody else within at least 50 yards that I had left the car vulnerable to a thief.

"You haven't locked the ****** doors!" he bawled. As soon as his voice died away he realised what he had said. He froze with panic as the possible consequences of his lapse sank in.

"I'm sorry, I'm sorry," he burbled desperately. "I forgot. I didn't mean to swear." I told him straight what I thought of him making a public spectacle of himself. It was... it was... well.... gross.

WHY I'M UNIQUE AMONG HUSBANDS

Mrs H has launched me into the new year with a rousing assessment of my last year's performance. She says that I am unique among fathers and husbands. When it comes to these two roles in family life, Mrs H says that I am in a class of my own. Isn't that lovely? I hear you say. No it isn't. You see, it's because I am not part of the herd that causes the problem. Consequently I am always being told what all the other husbands do, with the question, why do I not do likewise?

For instance, five days a week I come into the city to work. I spend a good proportion of my lunch hours buying, changing or searching for various things under Mrs H's direction. I have no desire, therefore, to continue this on a Saturday. Apparently you other husbands do.

"I don't know why you won't come in with us" admonishes Mrs H. "Other husbands take their families shopping on a Saturday. And they take them for lunch while they are at it."

It doesn't end there. You other creeps are at it all the time. While I am fighting a losing battle with the weedkiller in the drive, you lot are digging yours up and re-laying it. As I am planning the best way to fill a small crack in the plaster, "other husbands" are constructing extensions, knocking down walls and refurbishing kitchens.

Don't think I don't know who you are. I've seen you in the DIY store with your trolley loaded with bags of cement and bundles of wood. "When can you deliver the bathroom suite?" I hear you asking. "I was hoping to get on with that on Sunday". I am the one at the back of the queue with the small bottle of brush-cleaner.

At your wife's first sneeze, I am reliably informed that you other wimps cancel all arrangements for the day to look after the children while the little woman repairs to her bed to recuperate. Me? Apparently, all I do is to make less than sympathetic noises and vanish to work as usual, leaving "me to drag myself to school to drop off the Brats. Do it all again in the afternoon to collect them. And you still expect your tea when you come home from work."

I well remember when Celia's husband re-laid the patio, Mrs H said that ours needed doing as well. "Of course" she commented, "I told Celia you'd never be able to do that. You're hopeless when it comes to doing anything practical". This is, of course, perfectly true. The trouble is, I suffer from the fact that familiarity breeds acceptance.

We had a couple of dripping taps a while back. Because of my delay in getting new washers, the whole family got quite accustomed to screwing the taps practically into the basin to stop them dripping. Also, they thought nothing of having to use two hands to turn on the water when they wanted to wash their hands.

Visitors adapted similarly to the fruits of my procrastination. There were some good soakings when the washers were finally replaced and those unaware were still putting enormous effort in cranking-on the water.

To be fair, a scheme to replace the radiators in two of the bedrooms, which had been in the Fortress refurbishment plan for some considerable time, was successfully completed last year. A neighbour came round to give me a hand. He helped me with the plumbing. Well, all right, he actually did the plumbing. OK, OK, if you want to be precise, he did the work. I was allowed to help move the furniture and sweep up the mess afterwards.

In exasperation one day, I went up to Mrs H and put my arms round her and gave her a big kiss. "There," I said, "Do other husbands do that as well as I do?" I do feel that twinkle in her eye calls for some sort of explanation.

HOLDING THE LINE CAN BE TOUGH

We have found a use for Brat Major. She is proving ideal as a telephone answering machine. She is polite to callers, unlike her attitude to her parents. However, she does have enough loyalty not to tell whoever is on the phone if they have caught you with your trousers down.

When the phone rang the other night, she leapt to answer it and announced that it was GBH from across the road for Mrs H asking if we were going to the PTA disco on the Saturday night. Mrs H is rarely available to come to the phone immediately. So busy is she directing the operations of Fortress life that there is always a delay before she can get there.

When you have to "hold the line please" these days, you often get tinny music played down the phone to you. At Fortress Haverson you get me. I am dispatched to engage the caller in conversation.

Safe in the knowledge that I was out of reach, I was able to say more or less what I liked to GBH. Realising that I would have a live confrontation with her sooner or later, I backed off. I suggested to her that she might live up to her reputation if I wasn't careful.

"Oh I'm not like that any more" she said unconvincingly.

"Don't tell me you have somehow become a nice person" I responded, with more than a hint of sarcasm. She then called me a name which I will not mention here. Suffice it to say that there is paperwork in existence to prove her assertion otherwise.

At this point Mrs H began her voyage from the kitchen to the phone, a distance of about 12 yards. This follows a familiar pattern. Knowing that she will be on the phone for a time of indeterminate length, she punctuates her journey with words of motivation, guidance and correction to sustain the rest of us through the ensuing unsupervised period. There is always added emphasis on one word.

"Neil! KEEP an eye on that saucepan which is on the stove. DON'T let it boil over". Three more paces and it's "Aren't you two ready for bed YET?" Five yards from the phone: "All right, who has left the toilet light on AGAIN?" Two more yards and she stumbles over Brat Major's recorder. I'll leave you to work out for yourselves what she says here.

Finally she arrives at the phone and whoever is on the other end gets to hear the final instruction, and it's nearly always the same.

"Will you all please be QUIET," and she adds, as if we didn't all know, "I'm on the TELEPHONE!" She says this because, by now, Brat Major has retrieved her recorder and is instantly inspired to play it. Brat Minor has come across his aeroplane collection and is simulating the second world war with full sound effects.

Of course, on the odd occasion the call is for me. At the sound of "Dad, it's for you". I am there in seconds. Mostly it is some enthusiastic gentleman trying to persuade me that civilisation as we know it will cease if I do not invest money I do not have in his life assurance scheme.

If it happens to be a chum and I get gassing a la Mrs H, her face keeps appearing through the kitchen door mouthing words designed to speed me up. I have become quite a good lip-reader. I can cope with this but what does annoy me is when it is a mutual friend and she wants to throw in her five penn'orth. She hears half a conversation and starts shouting her contributions at me. I end up trying to hold two conversations at once and making a mess of both.

By the way GBH got her come-uppance for calling me a name on the phone. On the stagger home from the PTA disco she fell over. Twice.

TROUBLE WITH A FAILING MEMORY

Her mind has finally gone. Well, almost anyway. I have been monitoring Mrs H recently, and some of the things she has been doing, are bizarre to say the least.

I know that we all forget things. I have admitted in the past that I arrive at the garden shed and even as I unlock the door I realise I have completely forgotten the purpose of my journey. Until, that is, I have locked the door and returned indoors.

Sometimes I will be watching television when for no apparent reason I'll remember something that I have to do the following day. I have been known to go out to the garage and pin a note on the steering wheel of the car as a reminder for the morning

Mrs H is well beyond this stage. If you don't believe what I have to tell, I shall quite understand. If I had not witnessed some of the incidents myself I wouldn't give it credence either. Mrs H freely admits it all and puts it down to being pre-menopause or to early senile dementia.

It started with a relatively straightforward incident. Chatting to a long-standing friend in the village about their respective offspring, Mrs H suddenly exclaimed, "Oh I've forgotten the name of your daughter!" Well, OK, we all do things like that, but worse was to follow.

While out shopping a few days later, she rushed into a bakers, thankfully not in the village, and simply froze. "Oh!" she exclaimed, "Oh, I've forgotten what I came in here for." The helpful assistant enquired whether there was any possibility that it could have been a loaf of bread. A blushing Mrs H ordered a small wholemeal and ran.

More followed. We have lived in the same village for over 12 years. No problem, you might think, if someone asked Mrs H the way. She was on the telephone giving animated directions to someone on how to get to Fortress Haverson. She was reeling off street names. Well, most of them. "Then you turn into ... oh ... oh dear... I can't remember the name of the road where our cul-de-sac is off".

Three incidents then took place in the kitchen. She decided to take a break from the rigours of running Fortress H and sat down to have a piping hot cup of coffee. As she savoured her first sip, she felt bound to say to herself that the flavour was not all it might be. On closer inspection she spotted that she had all the ingredients in the cup except the coffee itself.

Cursing, she hurled the cup of sweet hot water down the sink, put some coffee and more sugar in the cup and refilled the kettle. She stomped off to perform some vital task or other, then returned, poured the water into the cup and sat down for another attempt at a quick break from her labours. One sip was all it took to have her spitting out her beverage. Cold coffee. She had forgotten to switch on the kettle.

Two similar occurrences show a lack of co-ordination somewhere. She delved into a cupboard and emerged with an armful of casseroles. With a puzzled look, she peered beyond where they had stood, then turned to me. "Where on earth are all my casseroles?" she asked with genuine bewilderment. Just what do you say to someone clutching to their bosom the very thing for which they are searching. Especially as only days before she had done the same thing with the potato peeler.

When I found the mat for the bathroom basin pedestal in the toilet and the toilet mat in the bathroom, I accused her of doing it on purpose. I expected her to show some concern, but she just shook with near-hysterical laughter.

It's not me I fear for; it's the children. I mean, suppose she takes them somewhere and forgets to go back and pick them up. I don't know though. Perhaps there could be an up side to this after all.

PLASTIC SMILES IN A MOMENT OF TERROR

A further success in his weapon training was achieved by Brat Minor last Sunday. He outwitted the security of the Household Cavalry. Actually it was more luck than anything.

We attended the Household Cavalry's open day which they stage every year at Bodney near Watton, as part of their summer camp. As you enter the car park, selected cars are hived off for a security search. It was as the friendly policeman waved us through the gate that Brat minor, to our absolute horror, produced his cap gun. Whilst, on closer inspection, it is obviously a toy, to a suspicious soldier watching out for a terrorist attack, it could well have had the inmates of Fortress Haverson looking down the wrong end of a machine gun.

"Quick, stick it in the glove box," I shouted frantically as we headed towards an unsuspecting trooper".

"That's no good," yelled Mrs H, "In fact that's worse if we hide it, they'll think we are trying to smuggle it in."

"Shall I hold it up so they can see it?" piped up the owner of the pistol.

"No!" For once Mrs H and I were in perfect accord as our joint reply echoed around the car. We could see that they had finished searching a couple of cars and either us or the next vehicle would be waved aside to be frisked. "Put it under your coat but be careful how you get it out if we get stopped" was the best we could come up with.

We proceeded cautiously. The solder peered into the car. His gaze was met by four faces each sporting a huge plastic smile, trying to signal that here was one innocent happy family out to enjoy themselves and without any thoughts of blowing up the Mounted Regiment of the Household Cavalry.

It worked. Clearly the sight of four grinning idiots was too much for him and, hurriedly, he waved us through. Our ordeal wasn't over. Having cleared this hurdle the young terrorist was brandishing his gun quite openly. He was invited to conceal it, sharpish, as we were approaching two more soldiers who were directing visitors into parking spaces. I drew the car to a halt and we sat there with our artificial smiles well in place until several more cars had parked. When the coast was clear, Brat Minor was ushered from the car like a suspect and, flanked by me and Brat Major, he was escorted to the boot of the car where the gun was locked away for the day.

Brat Minor argued later that, since he had been told to take something to amuse him in the car, bearing in mind where he was going, the gun seemed   a logical choice.

If we are going out, we do always try and make sure the Brats have something with which to amuse themselves, particularly on long journeys. If they don't have something to do, they turn to that well-known pastime of sibling baiting. This leads inevitably to arguments and they end up straining to nip, punch or hang each other by the seat belt. Mrs H starts yelling at them to calm down and I shout my usual "If I have to stop this car ..." This sentence always remains unfinished, as I am never quite sure exactly what I would do to them if I did stop.

Mind you, it can be just as bad if they do take something with which to occupy themselves. We had to ban Brat Minor's hand-held Thunderbirds game when I became homicidal after 15 miles of infernal bleeping as he successfully vaporised marauding aliens.

As for the cassettes they insist on having played, I am word perfect in practically every Roald Dahl story that has been committed to tape. And being cocooned on the A11 with Brat Major's throbbing reggae tape is enough to make you confess the darkest of secrets.

Perhaps I should offer the Brat's services to the Household Cavalry. An hour in the car with them would break the toughest of prisoners.

THE WRONG PLACE AT THE WRONG TIME

You may recall a couple of months ago, I mentioned that Mrs H operates an office desk from the top of the bread bin. She keeps a diary there plus all unanswered letters and unpaid bills. I was amazed how many women subsequently confessed also to using the top of their bread bin as a filing cabinet. Well, we have had a couple more belters from the Department of Female Logic whose headquarters I am wholly convinced is based at Fortress Haverson. I was making a sandwich. I chose the kitchen work surface as the exact location to construct my snack.

"What on earth do you think you are doing?" barked a familiar voice from behind me. I leapt in surprise, almost adding a couple of fingers to the filling of my sandwich as I sliced the bread. What was I doing wrong? I wasn't using white bread; haven't seen any of that in the house for years. Not since we entered our fibre period.

"Just making a sarnie. Why?" I replied, brain still whirring away. What could it be? It wasn't near a meal time and there was plenty of butter.

"You're using the worktop!" she exclaimed. At this point I knew I was beaten. Where else should I make a sandwich? In the bath?

"I've just cleaned it to do some cooking" she pointed out with exasperation. Of course, how stupid of me. The work top is for preparing food. Hang on, though, wasn't that what I was doing? Oh well, no point in arguing. I seized all my bits and headed for the kitchen table.

"Not on there! You'll have crumbs everywhere." Does this mean that we will no longer sit at the table to eat in case we make a mess? How about the garage? I can always back the car out at meal times.

"If you must make a sandwich, do it quickly then I'll clean the surface again." I headed back the way I had come. "Not down that end!" Now what? "So it's you who has the bread out near the bread bin and puts crumbs in all my papers."

I have to say that by now the desire for a sandwich was waning, not to mention the feeling of absolute guilt at using the kitchen for the purpose for which I had always believed it was there. This made me realise that this is not the first time this way of thinking has been peddled around Fortress H. Washing one's hands also springs to mind. For this purpose we have a sink in the kitchen and a sink in the bathroom. No problem. Well, perhaps sometimes there is. You see, we're not always allowed to use them. I will come in from the garden after a good weeding session   and head for the kitchen sink to remove the soil.

"You can't wash your hands in there. Can't you see I've just cleaned it ready to do some hand-washing?" Fair enough. Off to the bathroom. "Do you have to wash your hands in there?" Now what? There is soap and running water available. "I've just cleaned the bathroom. You know we've got John and Celia coming round tonight. I don't want you going in there and messing up the sink. Can't you just wait and use the kitchen sink when I've finished?"

Great. Can't wash my hands. She'll go berserk if I touch anything with dirty hands so I must sit quietly in the corner until I am allowed to do my ablutions.

The clincher comes when I am finally allowed to scrub up. With hands dripping wet, I reach for - guess what? Yes - the towel. "Don't use that. It's a clean towel just out. I know what your hands are like after you have been in the garden, even though you say you've washed them." Of course, towels are only there for show, not to actually dry your hands.

And another thing, just what am I supposed to do while I am waiting for a sink to become free so I can wash my hands? I suppose I could always make a sandwich.

READY FOR ANYTHING AT THE FORTRESS

I do worry about Mrs H. Yes, I know I go on about this but I am sure the grey matter continues to decay at an alarming rate.

She was in fine form the other night. She was off out for the evening. Life becomes extremely tense on occasions like this. The rest of us are abandoned totally while Mrs H devotes all her energies to getting ready. This is an operation driven by panic. She is rather like the white rabbit in Alice in Wonderland, muttering continually that she will be late. Except I doubt whether the white rabbit was in danger of missing his appointment with the duchess because he couldn't find the butterfly clasp that went with his right ear-ring.

Last minute instructions were belted out as she headed out of the house. I followed her like an obedient Labrador, receiving updates on my orders all the way to the car. I was standing in the Fortress drive seeing her out when, through the gloom, I spotted that our next door neighbour's car door was open. I popped round to tell him. He swiftly pointed out that his wife had been shopping and must have forgotten to close it after she had unloaded. We indulged in a swift exchange about the pressures these poor old wives and mothers are under which causes them to have these mental aberrations.

Mrs H then proceeded to confirm the point for us. She had installed herself in the car and started the engine. The headlights came up, she revved the engine and swept out of the drive. As I waved goodbye, I thought that something did not look quite right. She had travelled only a couple of hundred yards when there was a thud. She braked immediately and I ran after her. Through the dark, I could just pick out something lying in the road. At first I thought she had hit a cat but then I realised it was a shoe. Mrs H alighted from the vehicle anxiously.

"Have you got it?" she asked as I stood there hoping none of the other residents would be peeping from behind their curtains looking at that strange couple from up the road. He in his slippers clutching a lady's suede shoe and she marching toward him as if he was holding the crown jewels.

"It's a shoe" I exclaimed.

"I know" wailed Mrs H irritably. "I've got the other one here. I left them on the roof of the car as I was putting the key in the door." She retrieved her footwear and headed back to the car, adding "I must have forgotten them and driven off". With that she was back in the driving seat and on her way as if it happened all the time.

Perhaps it does. Some women drivers do seem to go armed with a pair of shoes for any eventuality. A pair for driving, a pair for walking round the shops and a pair in case they have a chance meeting with Royalty.

I will say that Mrs H is trying to reactivate the brain. She has embarked on some adult education, taking a course in computers. She is learning all about a personal computer application called Windows but I have to say that there is some way to go yet. "I'm really enjoying this" she told me after her third session. Seeing my quizzical look she added, "You know, learning all about Mirrors". Glass, mirrors, windows, I suppose it's all the same really.

What worries me most is that it may be inherent, that she may have passed it on to Brat Minor. Ask him what he did at school that day and it's gone, history. His young mind has moved on to other things and it takes sustained churning of the cerebral cogs for him to recall what he was doing an hour ago, let alone during craft, design and technology.

You may be wondering what our children have inherited from their father. Not much as far as I can see. They don't do what their mother tells them whereas, of course, I always do. And they complain about her cooking whereas I daren't.

Mind you, if Brat Major develops jodhpur thighs, that certainly isn't anything to do with me.

THE NIGHT I BECAME
TRULY MY OWN MAN

I did it. I did it. I asserted myself and got my own way.

Well, almost. This major coup was achieved over the simple matter of what to wear. As a rule, if we are going out, I seek advice on what to wear, get it out of the wardrobe, put it on then I am told to change into something completely different because "I don't like it now I've seen it on."

Last Saturday was different. Our old friend GBH was hosting a gathering and we were off for a couple of sherbets and a bite to eat. Dress was optional but a veiled threat had been issued by the hostess to dress up a bit. This suited me as I do prefer to wear something other than jeans if we are going out. Mrs H made it quite clear that she preferred me in jeans and a particular sweatshirt.

In a bold act of defiance, I decided to put on something smarter. Of course, after all these years I didn't have the confidence to fly solo, so I informed Mrs H that I would need guidance in selecting an appropriate shirt to go with my trousers. Nothing more was said so, continuing my new-found independence, I got out my gear for the evening. I selected a pair of black trousers, a beige-coloured shirt which had been approved in the past for wearing with the black trousers and a tie that Mrs H had bought me to go with that very shirt. I couldn't go wrong and I was being my own man.

Nothing more was said until we were in the throes of getting ready. On one of her many trips between bathroom and bedroom, Mrs H paused briefly to mention that she had spotted some of my clothes on the bed but assumed that they could not possibly be what I intended wearing that evening. On hearing that they were she again made her feelings plain.

"You know what I think you should wear but if you are dressing up, surely you are not wearing that shirt, and the tie is so boring". I pointed out that she had chosen most of my ties so did this comment apply to her entire selection? She replied with something quite profound.

"That tie you've chosen is all right for work. If you are going out you need a tie that makes a statement".

Yes, I'll let you know if I work that one out.

And so it was that we arrived at GBH's for me to be told by the hostess that I looked smart in my navy trousers, white shirt and multi-coloured tie. What's that? What happened to the black trousers, beige shirt and boring tie? Well, all right, Mrs H did make a few minor adjustments to my choice but don't forget, I didn't wear jeans.

It was a bit worrying to be told also by the hostess that I smelt nice. It just struck me that it was said in such a way that it was a refreshing change and that I usually smelt like Brat Minor. Mrs H can claim credit for a fragrant Haverson. She provides me with anything that needs dabbing or spraying about the person.

In between discarding my choice of outfit and putting on Mrs H's modified ensemble, I had been ordered to offer obscure parts of the body at which small amounts of sociably acceptable smelling liquids were squirted. I was told to wash off all the different smellies leaving clean skin to receive the chosen fragrance.

The point is, I forgot to do this, which meant that when Mrs H proudly announced to a crowded kitchen what the particular eau de Haverson was, it could in fact have been any one of about five, and depended on whether you were standing up or downwind and to which part of the Haverson extremities you were adjacent at the time.

The only thing that worries me about this is that, prior to the event, GBH had threatened to cajole me into dancing with her. Now, the mental scars have barely healed from the last encounter. Anyway, no mention was made of this dance all evening until we left, when GBH shouted at my retreating figure "I still owe you".

What stopped her? Was it because I wasn't as smart as I thought I was? Or was she put off the scent, so to speak, by the aroma of my combined range of body sprays? Hang on, there's an even worse possibility. Perhaps I do smell like Brat Minor.

FAITHFUL SLIPPER CARRIER,
THAT'S ME

I cannot deny heaving a sigh of relief some mornings when I make good my escape from Fortress Haverson and head for work. I leave behind the dawn chorus of Mrs H inviting the Brats to "pack your school bags now or else!"

There is the odd phone call that comes in now and again to update my daily orders but otherwise I am not involved in domestic matters until I return home in the evening.

On a clear, crisp lunchtime recently, I was wandering aimlessly around the city and nothing was further from my thoughts than the struggle for survival at Fortress H. Suddenly I felt a tug at my arm. I recoiled instantly. Thinking I was about to be mugged I thrust a protective hand round my wallet. But it was much worse. It was Mrs H. My hand stayed on my wallet.

She was on a spontaneous shopping spree and had spotted me taking the air. Immediately I concocted some story about having just popped out for a break from the daily toil to buy some de-icer. This was to avoid being dragged into the "I just want you to look at a dress and tell me if it suits me" situation.

"Oh, I'll walk with you" came the instant reply. All attempts to shake her off failed and, since she had bought me a couple of shirts in the course of her spending, I walked on, slipping easily into listening mode. A colleague saw us and said to me later that I appeared to be sporting a somewhat glazed look. This was due to the fact that I was absorbing the "I should have bought it when I saw it 'cos when I went back it was gone" scenario.

This return visit after Mrs H has seen something is sometimes given to me to execute. In fact, on a recent excursion my true worth as a husband was highlighted by a lady from Marks and Spencers' shoe department. I was sent on this particular mission with the following instructions "First floor, ladies' shoes, left hand side. Pair of slippers, beige with gold edging, size 5, reduced to £5.99".

I zoomed in to the store, found the right display and stared at it for a few seconds. I spotted what looked like the objects of Mrs H's desire and took them to the counter. I produced from my pocket the piece of paper which had the details on and read it to the assistant, expecting immediate confirmation that I had carried out my task successfully.

"Well" she said doubtfully, "they look more cream than beige and the gold isn't exactly round the edge. In fact it is everywhere but the edge. Why don't we go and have another look?"

Like a chastised child, I followed her meekly to the slipper stand. There, right beside the ones I had picked, were the slippers which unmistakable matched Mrs H's description. In fact they were touching each other as if they had been vying for my custom. We retraced our steps to the cash till with me feeling somewhat humble.

"At least" I rallied pathetically, "I got the right store" and then she said it, the comment that now I use to tell Mrs H how lucky she is to have such an obliging husband as me.

"I think you are very good to come in and get them" she said sweetly. I fell instantly in love with her and asked her to put her testimonial in writing on the back of the receipt. Sadly a queue had formed and Mrs H has to take my word that such a tribute was paid to me.

I wonder if she really appreciates me. Take the time some years ago when I was sent to pick up Brat Major after she had been appearing in a dance show. The brief was clear. "Stay with her until she is changed, make sure she doesn't leave anything behind". On arrival at the hall, I enquired where I would find her and was directed through a door. I swept in and was confronted by not only Brat Major but about 50 other females of all age groups and in various states of undress. Imagine my dilemma. Should I beat a hasty retreat or, like the faithful old retainer I am, carry out Mrs H's instructions?

There was only one choice. The things I put myself through for that woman.

PLAYING FOR TIME
WITH A BIN BAG

I have locked antlers with Brat Major. It has reached the stage where neither of us will give in and I must confess I can't quite see how it is going to finish. I took up the cudgel on behalf of Mrs H and now find myself the big baddie of the piece.

The issue was yet again the state of the young lady's bedroom and her refusal to tidy it up. Mrs H had reached the stage of breaking out into a mild sweat when she called me in as back-up. The aforementioned bedroom looked like the aftermath of a jumble sale. Its young occupant could see no reason why she should bring some semblance of order to what she asserted was her domain. She went to some lengths to point out that, as far as she was aware, there were no visitors expected to Fortress Haverson so no one except her family would see it and "who cares about them?"

I decided to take a positive parental attitude. I gave her half an hour to begin tidying up or I would consign all the extraneous matter to the bin. That should do it, I thought, but I hadn't bargained on the strength of determination of the rebel. I think she gets in from her mother, you know. After the period of grace had expired, I confronted her with the ultimatum that if she didn't start right now I would become active with a bin liner and soon have the job done for her.

Still no action, so I set about my task. She smiled with satisfaction as her school pencil case hit the sack. She positively purred as her clarinet book went in, but the smile faded as her cherished velvet hat disappeared and there was mild panic when her Take That cassettes were flung heartlessly after the rest of her rubbish.

It was about this time that I became concerned with the hint of a smile which Mrs H had on her lips, as she ghosted in and out of the scene. She pointed out that Brat Major would not give a hoot at the loss of her dressing gown, and just what was I going to do with all that stuff if there was no compromise?

By now I was too far committed to my crusade to back down,

and marched triumphantly downstairs with my swag. I placed it at the back door to await a ceremonial disposing of the superfluous assets of Brat Major. She'll crack soon, I thought. She'll be crawling around me to have her goodies back, promising to put them all away. She still didn't cave in. The bag of booty languished at the back door like a suspect package awaiting the attention of the bomb squad. Mrs H attempted to bail me out by buying me some time.

"Put it in   the boot of the car. We'll take it somewhere and sell it" she said for all to hear. Relieved at this temporary reprieve, I hastened to the garage and stashed it in the boot of the car. It was still there the following day. Later I was in the village with the enemy and bumped into our former neighbour, the lovely GBH. I have to say that even she was supportive of me when Brat Major told the tale.

"Let me have it" demanded GBH, "it can go in the school jumble sale next Saturday. If you want your bits and pieces" she advised Brat Major "you can come to the sale and buy them back".

"Ah ha! That'll teach you" I cackled to my confused daughter. I thought about this later and went decidedly off the idea. Brat Major's possessions had been purchased in the first place mainly with money supplied by me. If she was to buy them back, she would have to use her pocket money. That also is extorted from me. Therefore, to make my point about her untidiness, I would be paying twice for the wretched stuff.

So how do I get out of this stalemate? I know the sack is not so full as it was. I did spot a small human dart past the window the other day, returning minutes later following the sound of a car boot lid slamming shut. Shortly after this the velvet hat and the Take That tapes became part of her life again. Even her pencil case was retrieved, but this was probably more in fear of retribution at school then concern about the wrath of her demented father.

The trouble is, I saw her with a bin liner the other day. I fear she may have taken a peep at the state of my corner of the master bedroom. What's that expression, hoist by one's own petard?

ESCAPING TO A WORLD
ALL OF MY OWN

Mrs H has accused me of anti-social habits. Now, before you get the wrong idea, I must point out that she is not referring to anything unsavoury here. It's not such things as leaving the loo seat up or making a cheese sandwich without washing my hands after I have been cleaning out the drains.

This all surrounds a small investment I made in some equipment to enhance what little leisure time I manage to salvage from the daily struggle at Fortress H. I have bought myself a set of headphones for the hi-fi. This has opened up a whole new world for me.

Usually, if I put on my boring 60s music, I get told to turn it down. It is intrusive. Of course, if Mrs H wants the wretched Rolling Stones on it is different. Their output, apparently, gains a greater quality if it is played at such volume that the speakers vibrate.

I was having a classical session in the armchair the other night, with my head completely full of The Arrival of the Queen of Sheba. I was oblivious to the rest of life. Suddenly, I became aware of some violent activity a few yards way. As my glazed eyes focused I realised it was a fellow human being leaping around like a demented wallaby, trying to attract my attention. Arms waving, mouth contorting, it was Mrs H wishing to communicate. I slipped one ear free to listen to Mrs H, allowing the Queen of Sheba to continue to make her good entrance through the other. I was informed, through my exposed ear, that I would shortly be required to lend assistance in the kitchen or my meal would never be ready. I nodded enthusiastically and returned to my musical retreat.

I must say that it was really rather nice in this cocooned world. Every so often a Brat would appear and mouth something to me. I smiled happily and nodded benevolently at them. I watched their retreating backs as they disappeared to the strains to Dvorak, blissfully unaware that they had been seeking permission to do all sorts of things contrary to Fortress guidelines. In my reverie I had given grinning acquiescence to their requests.

Time stood still on my musical desert island and, before I knew it, the demented wallaby returned and began making red-faced gestures at me. Reluctantly I halted the 1812 Overture just prior to the cannons. There were enough bullets flying around as it was. I dragged myself off to assist with the fatigues and received a lecture on how anti-social my new hobby is.

Once I had completed my tasks to the satisfactory standard, I returned to my headphones. As I wallowed in a bit of Greig I decided to close my eyes in the hope of giving out a "Gone Fishin'" message. At least I wouldn't be able to see the demented wallaby if it returned to the room having histrionics. As I conducted the orchestra, I ruminated on the anti-social habits of my fellow inmates. In my humble view, what I was doing paled into insignificance in comparison to them.

Can a room actually be anti-social? There is Brat Minor's well-known squat for a start. It ought to have a government health warning on the door. As for its occupant, he would be a more welcome member of the human race if he could be persuaded that the white lump on the side of the bath is supposed to be used in conjunction with the hot water in which he is wallowing, to cleanse his disgusting little body.

As for both their eating habits, they leave something to be desired. They are supplied with a knife and fork, but it seems that the quality of chips is improved if they are stuffed into the eager mouth with thumb and fingers. And when Brat Minor scoffs his dessert, the room echoes to the sound of his teeth rattling on the spoon as if he were trying to eat that too.

There is, of course, that fourth member of the family, the one who cranks up the hair dryer, when I am engrossed in a particularly tense thriller on television, then asks to be brought up to date when she has finished so I miss a crucial part of the plot while I am giving a resumé.

Perhaps it would not be in my best interests to mention anything about her. I may have to retire to the sanctuary of the headphones. I'd rather have my eardrums blasted by Mozart than Mrs H.

OUR DREAMS AT AGE 16
SOMETIMES COME TRUE

One of the many worries that any parent has must be surely, what the children will do when they grow up. Will they become New Age Travellers, partake of free love and indulge in illegal substances? Or will they conform and become accountants and secretaries? Thankfully, Mrs H and I have had our minds put at rest about one of our offspring at least. The other night, Brat Major sombrely announced her blueprint for her own future. This is it.

Life will, apparently, change direction when she is 16. Her intention is to leave home and get a flat. She will become a journalist, have her hair permed and her ears pierced. The final coup de grace is that she will invest in two hamsters. The thinking behind this, in spite of the fact that it is from a female, is quite logical. The journalist bit is to write exposés about her father to get her own back. The rest is what she sees as freedom from the shackles of the parental control.

According to her, Mrs H and I are unique as parents in the way in which we hold her in a vice-like grip while her chums lead lives of unbridled freedom. If we were to believe her, every other girl in her class has curly hair, had their ears pierced at birth and has a veritable zoo of caged pets.

I cannot remember what I wanted to do when I was 16. It would almost certainly have involved some kind of ball game. I seem to recall that girls were strange creatures that prevented my mates from playing cricket and caused them to do uncharacteristic things like wash their hair and go out for tea on Sundays. Some things don't change.

Intrigued by Brat Major's revelation, I conducted a survey of the family.

Brat Minor's aspirations were quite straightforward but, for a male, quite illogical. For some reason he wants to open a coffee shop. I do not think that his decision is based on any research he has done into exploiting a niche in the market with a view to capitalising on a consumer need. It's probably more to do with having access to an endless supply of Coke and sticky buns.

I asked Mrs H if she could remember what she had wanted to do when she was 16. She paused from her toil and allowed her mind to deviate from its thoughts of such critical issues as whether to wash her hair before she did the ironing or afterwards. "I think I wanted to be a fashion buyer" she mused, staring pensively out of the window. Her daughter would probably argue that Mrs H lacks the ability to do this judging by a comment madam made the other day.

Mrs H had bought her a new outfit which turned out to be too big. However, it fitted Mrs H so she decided to have it herself. Brat Major told me this and confided with some relief "Thank goodness Mum is going to keep it. At last she'll have some modern clothes to wear when I'm out with her. It's so embarrassing!" Mind you, it did cross my mind what Mrs H might do if she saw an 11-year old coming the other way wearing the same outfit.

Anyway, I thought I had a fair idea of what Mrs H would have dreamt about when she was 16 so I filled in the blanks for her. "I think you probably wanted to find yourself a handsome young man. One who would be an attentive husband and a perfect father to your children. Someone who would wake you in the morning and make sure you eventually got up. Eject spiders and swat flies when they strayed into your comfort zone.

"Someone who would not look puzzled when you changed the rules without prior warning and would present a face that showed he was absolutely riveted when you rabbit on about whether to wear leggings or a skirt to help at the school fete.

"How you must have fallen asleep at night dreaming about someone who would wait patiently in the street while you wrestled with a contact lens and who would smile benignly when the solutions for cleaning those lenses leapt from the bathroom cabinet and struck him a painful blow on the side of the head.

"You must have gone starry-eyed at the thought of finding someone who would operate within your time warp and not Greenwich Mean Time. And who would smack his lips enthusiastically when served the Aubergine Bake."

Well, even if Brat Major's dreams don't come true, at least Mrs H's did.

What EDP readers said about
Neil's weekly column...

SHEILA GREENACRE
Knyvett Green
Ashwellthorpe
Norwich

Dear Sir
Re Neil Haverson's column (EDP May 1), Mrs
H's sister, with whom I worked for some
years, will confirm that, on numerous
occasions, I have commented on the uncanny
similarities between Fortress Haverson and
the Greenacre Garrison, which is inhabited
by three brats.
The reason for my putting pen to paper on
this occasion, however, is the bread bin!
It was only this week, after months of
searching for the right one, that I
eventually acquired a replacement for the
rust-ridden health hazard that served as a
bread bin in our house.
As I removed the new one from its box, my
husband gave a triumphant snigger, but it
was not until I installed it in position
that I realised why - the new shape meant
that no longer could your lunch boxes and
an ancient ice-cream tub full of out-of-
date vouchers live on top of the bread
bin, as it had a curved lid!
I got my own back, though - I put them
all in the cupboard, and when you open the
door they all fall out!

M.S. KERKHAM
Bailey Lane
Clenchwarton

Dear Sir
With reference to "Trouble with a failing
memory" by Neil Haverson (EDP, March 27);
reading to the point where "she had
forgotten to switch on the kettle",
reminds me that I have done all these
things.
In addition, I have searched for my
spectacles while I was wearing them and
put food into the airing cupboard instead
of the larder.

R.S. PRATT   (Mrs)
Old Yarmouth Road
Sutton

Dear Sir
Is there a real Mrs H or is she a figment
of Neil Haverson's imagination, and is he
really a bachelor who imagines family life
is how he writes?
I'm longing to know.   If there is a Mrs
H (complete with brats!), I bet she gets
very annoyed at his "ramblings" - I would!
Carry on Neil - I enjoy your column - real
or imagined.

BRIDGET CLARKE
Micklehaugh Farm
Banham

Dear Sir
Since Neil Haverson is inspiring such
commendations, should there not be an
Appreciation Society for Mrs H, with an
affiliated Brat pack.
Would it be appropriate for Blue Peter to
design a model of the Fortress, for
afficionados to make out of junk?
Any subscriptions could go to a legal
fund, should GBH wish to sue for libel
(provided, of course, this interest was
declared in the right quarters).

K C FAIRCLOTH
Hawthorn Drive
Dersingham

Dear Sir
Could Mrs Haverson be persuaded to
contribute a column to the EDP on the
subject of Fort Haverson?   There are two
sides to every question, and I am sure Mrs
H's would be interesting.
I'm blowed if I would let my husband say
things like that, in print, about me!
But perhaps Mrs H does not read the EDP.

ANDREW YOUNGS
Staithe Road
Bungay

Dear Sir
As a confirmed bachelor, I found Neil
Haverson's insight into the joys of
married life (December 10) most
illuminating.
The alacrity with which he describes the
fear instilled by his wife confirms
suspicions which I have long held
regarding the draconian restrictions on
personal liberty imposed by the married
condition.
Indeed, I would be most interested to hear
from any commentators as to why seemingly
level-headed chaps wish to subject
themselves to this form of psychological
torture with the apparent zeal and
enthusiasm of a bunch of lemmings.

K WINDEBANK
Merchant Way
Hellesdon

Dear Sir
I have enjoyed the EDP for many years, and
now my great delight is Saturday morning.
Mr Neil Haverson's column is wonderful,
but having read it from the start I, like
many others, want to know what Mrs H is
like.
All I can recall reading at anytime re her
appearance is "She worries about her heavy
thighs."   Couldn't we have a tiny
photograph?   If not, please Neil, a
little hint, dark, fair, short, tall?
Take pit on us before we die of curiosity
and an over-stretched imagination.
Thanks for a lovely column.